45 PEOPLE, PLACES' & EVENTS in Black History YOU SHOULD KNOW

Historical Profiles

By **Daniel J. Middleton**

UNIQUE
COLORING

Images that appear in this book are in the public domain unless otherwise stated. Bottom *Introduction* illustration based on a self-portrait courtesy of Oladimeji Ajegbile.

Edited by Karen Dyer and Naomi Middleton
Layout and Design by Daniel J. Middleton

First published in the United States
in December 2021 by Unique Coloring
Williamstown, New York

Printed by Ingram Book Group, LLC.

ISBN: 978-1-935702-46-7 (Paperback)
ISBN: 978-1-935702-47-4 (Hardcover)
ISBN: 978-1-935702-48-1 (eBook)

Library of Congress Control Number: 2021947380

1 2 3 4 5 6 7 8 9 10   IBG   25 24 23 22 21

VISIT US ONLINE:
www.uniquecoloring.com

Contents

45 PEOPLE, PLACES, & EVENTS in Black History YOU SHOULD KNOW

Other Books by

Daniel J. Middleton

The Black History Activity Book
Articles, Coloring Pages, Puzzles, and More

21st Century Black Changemakers
Biography Coloring

2022–2024 Monthly Planner
Colorable Three-Year Black History Calendar

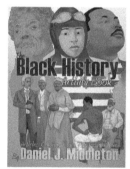

Find them at
www.uniquecoloring.com

UNIQUE
COLORING

Introduction

Banner image features an illustration of correspondence representing a primary research source.

I n the following pages, I present the history of 45 fascinating and lesser-known subjects that have made an indelible mark on black culture and the world. These biography entries run the gamut from entertainers like John W. Bubbles (the father of rhythm tap) to anomalies like Covert, Michigan, a town that never segregated, despite the prevailing racist customs and laws of the day. You will learn about the hidden history of black colleges and universities and how they helped German Jewish scholars during the height of the Nazis. You will also meet talented artists and architects, brilliant inventors and medical professionals, gifted musicians, skilled athletes, and pioneering business owners, to name a few.

Arranged chronologically, *45 People, Places, and Events in Black History You Should Know* will guide you through a world rich with talent and creativity, inventive genius, endurance, and extraordinary determination. You will see how the past informs the present, which it has shaped, and you will come away with a new understanding of key yet hardly discussed historical events. More than 150 photos, images, and illustrations (mostly in color) accompany the text to help bring the subjects to life.

So with that, find a quiet, cozy spot, unwind, and spend some time relishing these 45 historical profiles.

Daniel J. Middleton
Author and Illustrator

TIME to STEP

Edisto Island
Home of the "Black Kings"

Banner image features black Union soldiers planting sweet potato on Edisto Island.

here is a little-known island in South Carolina named Edisto that has an interesting history. Following the Civil War, a few newly freed slaves who had been on the Sea Island made good on their freedom to the point where they were able to thrive, earning the nickname "the black kings of Edisto." One such "king" had a son named Henry Hutchinson, whose home, built in the late nineteenth century, stood next to Edisto's first black-owned cotton gin, which Henry ran. This was a sign of how much things had improved for ex-slaves on the island following the war. The two-story home, built with some Victorian flour-ishes, featured a big wraparound porch that gave Henry and his wife, Rosa Swinton Hutchinson, ample views of both their field and the marsh in the distance. It is now called the Henry Hutchinson House.

Henry and Rosa

The couple is seen riding in their shay. They were among the most prosperous blacks living on Edisto Island following the Civil War.

Edisto, which was originally occupied by the Edistow people, an Indig-enous sub-tribe of the Cusabo, soon saw an influx of white Colonial settlers in the seventeenth century. An entry by Ford Walpole in the *South Caroli-na Encyclopedia* reads:

> In the mid-1500s Spanish settlers arrived on the island they called 'Oristo' and established a Jesuit mission. Englishman Robert Sand-ford explored Edisto in 1666, and a decade later the 'Edistow' deeded the island to the Lords Proprietors. The Spanish raided an English settlement on Edisto in 1686, but Anglo settlers and their African slaves remained and increased in the ensuing decades."

Before 1700, the white settlers divided the island into tracts of land called plantations, on which they planted indigo, rice, and later cotton. Landowners also harvested timber and deerskins and herded cattle whose hides and salt beef were sold to the European market and Caribbean plantations, respectively.

With the success of the plantations, landowners grew rich following the American Revolution, and Edisto's sought-after Sea Island cotton brought them fame. Of course, all the labor was carried out by hundreds of enslaved blacks stolen from the African continent. They formed a Gullah community and developed a language known as Gullah or Geechee, which exists to this day.

Edisto Island

From the "Crisp Map" of 1711.

As the Civil War erupted, planters largely abandoned Edisto by November 1861, and within a month many remaining blacks managed to escape the few white masters left. These black escapees established refugee camps and took up arms. They even put up a resistance against a band of Confederate soldiers on a raid. Union forces were also stationed on the island for a time.

Henry's father, Jim Hutchinson, was the son of a female slave and an unidentified white man. Jim served in the Union Navy while they were stationed on Edisto. The presence of the Union soldiers forced more plantation owners to flee both their land and slaves. After the war, Jim Hutchinson became a leader of the black community and urged the people to acquire property on the island.

Jim eventually pooled resources with many of the freed slaves and, as a collective, purchased land on Edisto. Like any cooperative venture, each purchaser then owned a small interest in the acquired lands. Sadly, the Henry Hutchinson House is all that remains of this short-lived heyday in black history that lasted till around the end of Reconstruction. While it stood vacant for years, deteriorating in idleness for close to a century, Henry's descendants decided to sell the property, which consisted of ten or so undeveloped acres, to a land trust. That land trust aims to restore the home to its former glory and open it to the public. **U**

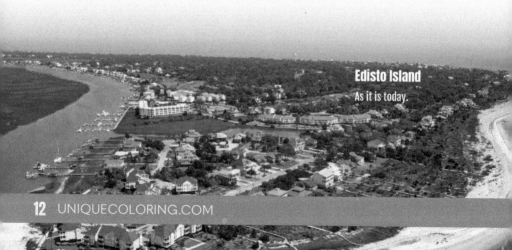

Edisto Island

As it is today.

Onesimus
The Black Boston Slave Who Helped Mitigate Smallpox

Banner image features a proposed Onesimus and a 1770 engraving of Boston Harbor.

A black slave named Onesimus, who was stolen from his West African homeland and brought by force to the Massachusetts Bay Colony where he was sold, became one of the most important Bostonians in history. Onesimus is credited with instituting the first recorded inoculations in the Americas, which later led to the development of the first vaccines close to a century later.

A celebrated New England minister named Cotton Mather—who had been involved in the Salem witch trials—was gifted with Onesimus in 1706 by his Puritan congregation. Onesimus, whose origins and birth name are unknown, received his name from Mather. Meaning "profitable," or "helpful," it was borrowed from the Greek name of a New Testament slave.

Smallpox had been ravaging the New England territory before the arrival of Onesimus, with Boston itself experiencing an outbreak in 1703. In examining his new property, Mather asked Onesimus if he had ever been infected with smallpox in his homeland. Onesimus gave a vague reply, saying "Yes and no," which demanded an explanation. Onesimus showed Mather his scar and went on to describe what he had experienced in Libya, something called variolation.

It involved taking infectious fluid like pus from smallpox patients. That infected material would then be inserted into a cut in the skin of a healthy person during a procedure supervised by a physician. If successful, the healthy person would experience mild smallpox symptoms before building up an immunity to the disease over time. But variolation was not always successful.

Looked at another way, this was the precursor of inoculation, where people are infected with a weakened form of a disease that allows their immune system to create a resistance to it via what is now called antibodies. Onesimus introduced this science to Mather, who

Cotton Mather
In full period dress.

went in search of evidence of its practice elsewhere. He found accounts that proved variations of the practice were in use throughout Asia and Africa, and that spurred him to launch a campaign to spread the adoption of variolation throughout Boston. But the city's physicians ignored his call to action, decrying his folly in listening to the ramblings of a slave.

Cargo ships had brought smallpox to Boston time and again, yet little could be done about it, aside from imposing quarantine measures and making unsuccessful attempts to treat infected victims. In April 1721, one ship in particular, the HMS *Seahorse*, pulled into Boston from Barbados with a crew who had survived a recent bout of smallpox. One sailor managed to spread the disease while in Boston, however, and thereafter several infected sailors caused others to contract it. One of the worst smallpox epidemics in the history of Boston was soon underway.

Encouraged by what he had learned from Onesimus, Mather made another attempt, this time mailing a pamphlet outlining his arguments for inoculation to a physician in Boston named Zabdiel Boylston. Dr. Boylston took Mather's points to heart and performed the procedure on his young son, his slave, and his slave's son. After experiencing mild smallpox symptoms, all three patients recovered. Despite the new outbreak, after several Bostonians learned of Dr. Boylston's experiment, they reacted with disdain, tossing rocks with threatening and insulting notes through Mather's front window.

Widespread resistance from town officials and sporadic violence on the part of the public prevented Dr. Boylston from inoculating more than 287 or so patients. Nearly half of Boston—roughly 11,000 people—became infected by smallpox. Of the 287 patients treated by Dr. Boylston (including Mather's son), only 2% died from smallpox. On the other hand, over 14% of those who had not been inoculated by Boylston, contracted smallpox and died.

The inoculation measures carried out in Boston, which lasted till the late eighteenth century, paved the way for the development of the first smallpox vaccine by English physician Edward Jenner in 1796, and the eventual eradication of smallpox altogether. Smallpox is the only disease that has been entirely wiped out. At the heart of that victory is Onesimus, a little-known slave who certainly lived up to the meaning of his name. **U**

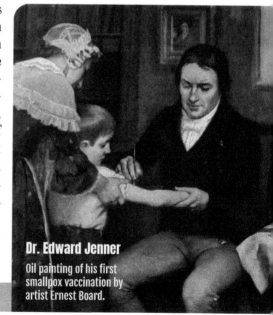

Dr. Edward Jenner

Oil painting of his first smallpox vaccination by artist Ernest Board.

Lucy Terry
omposer of the Oldest Existing Poem by a Black American

Banner image courtesy of artist Louise Minks and the Pocumtuck Valley Memorial Association, Deerfield, MA.

While Jupiter Hammon and Phillis Wheatley are credited as pioneering black poets, another black poet preceded them both in the annals of history with a piece that remained unpublished until 1855. Her name was Lucy Terry. Lucy's gift for storytelling was unparalleled. The one work that survives from her collective output is "Bars Fight," a 28-line narrative poem that recounts an attack on a colonial village by Abenaki natives. "Bars Fight" was composed in 1746, and the "Bars" referred to in the title is colonial-speak for a meadow, which was the setting for the attack in the Franklin County, Massachusetts village known as Deerfield.

Attack on Deerfield
Adapted illustration of Walter Henry Lippincott's original painting of a 1704 attack.

Lucy was present during the raid on the village that took place on August 25, 1746, and she witnessed firsthand the atrocities mentioned in her poem. Five white settlers were killed, one suffered mortal injuries, one escaped across a river, and another was taken captive to Canada. For over a century, Lucy's poem only enjoyed oral preservation, until it was published in a collection titled, *History of Western Massachusetts* by American poet and novelist Josiah Gilbert Holland. After its publication, however, "Bars Fight" fell into obscurity and was not rediscovered until 1942. That is the year the poem found its way into print a second time after almost another century. Lorenzo Greene, a history professor and author, published it in his book, *The Negro in Colonial New England 1620–1776.*

For many years, it was thought that Lucy put pen to paper when composing her poem, but recent scholarship suggests that, though she was literate, she may have relied on African oral tradition and merely recited what she had composed in her mind. Others in Deerfield Village later memorized and retold the epic poem and thereby kept both it and her name in remembrance. Support for this theory comes from the earliest known record of the poem in written form, which is traced to an 1819 lecture. This was followed by its first official printing in 1855.

Lucy Terry was born in Africa in 1724. She was kidnapped in childhood

Bars Fight
By Lucy Terry

August 'twas the twenty-fifth,
Seventeen hundred forty-six;
The Indians did in ambush lay,
Some very valiant men to slay,
The names of whom I'll not leave out.
Samuel Allen like a hero fout,
And though he was so brave and bold,
His face no more shall we behold.
Eleazer Hawks was killed outright,
Before he had time to fight—
Before he did the Indians see,
Was shot and killed immediately.
Oliver Amsden he was slain,
Which caused his friends much grief and pain.
Simeon Amsden they found dead,
Not many rods distant from his head.
Adonijah Gillett we do hear
Did lose his life which was so dear.
John Sadler fled across the water,
And thus escaped the dreadful slaughter.
Eunice Allen see the Indians coming,
And hopes to save herself by running,
And had not her petticoats stopped her,
The awful creatures had not catched her,
Nor tommy hawked her on her head,
And left her on the ground for dead.
Young Samuel Allen, Oh lack-a-day!
Was taken and carried to Canada.

and shipped to Bristol, Rhode Island. At only four years of age, Lucy was sold to Ebenezer Wells, a Deerfield, Massachusetts resident who owned a tavern in the village. Lucy was brought to live with Wells and his wife, who were childless. In 1735, during the Great Awakening, Lucy was baptized with the approval of Wells and she became a full church member in 1744, at the age of twenty. She remained a slave of the Wellses for another twelve years.

Her freedom came as a result of her marriage to a free black man named Abijah Prince, whom she wed in 1756. She was thereafter known as Lucy Prince. It is uncertain whether Wells released her from bondage or Abijah Prince purchased her freedom. In either case, Lucy was no longer a slave. The couple's first child was born in 1757, and they had five other children by 1769. They also moved to Guilford, Vermont in 1764. Two of their sons later served in the Revolutionary War.

Terry, who was known for her storytelling abilities since her youth, was also a seasoned orator. A white colonel named Eli Bronson once attempted to steal land from the Prince family by making false claims, and the case went before the Vermont Supreme Court. Despite hiring an attorney, Lucy, in a rare show of eloquence, successfully argued her case. She was opposed by two experienced litigators, one of whom was later elected chief justice. Lucy, who was the first woman to argue a case before Vermont's high court, was awarded $200.

Lucy Terry Prince passed away on July 11, 1821. She was a remarkable woman, and the respect paid to her in death is a testament to that fact. In Lucy's day, obituaries written for deceased females were notorious for their brevity and inaccuracy. When Lucy's obituary was read on Tuesday, August 21, 1821, it was unusually long and full of praise, as well as accurate details of her life. It was also printed in two papers, first in the *Vermont Gazette*, headquartered in Bennington, Vermont, and then in the *Franklin Herald* of Greenfield, Massachusetts. This highlights the level of importance Lucy commanded during her lifetime. A few lines from her obituary paint a clear picture of how she was regarded by those who came to know her:

> In this remarkable woman there was an assemblage of qualities rarely to be found among her sex. Her volubility was exceeded by none, and in general the fluency of her speech was not destitute of instruction and education. She was much respected among her acquaintances, who treated her with a degree of deference." U

Jean Baptiste Point du Sable
The First Settler and Founder of Chicago, Illinois

Banner image features a painting of Jean Baptiste Point du Sable by Ulrick Jean-Pierre.

Jean Baptiste Point du Sable was a pioneer and prominent trader of Haitian origin who, on October 25, 1968, was finally recognized as the founder of Chicago by city and state officials. He had been considered the city's first non-native settler since the 1850s, but many failed to honor him on the level of white pioneers until several decades after his death. Du Sable was also the first person to perceive the importance of Chicago, then called "Eschikagou," a Native American word used for smelly waters since the area carried the scent of wild onions. Chicago eventually grew from a small trading post to one of the largest cities in the United States. The city is now an important commercial center, but its success was borne out of du Sable's intimate relations with the native tribes, with whom he collaborated to lay the foundations of what would later become an important center of commerce, trade, and American industry.

Colony of St. Domingue

Tinted map of the island of St. Domingue (Haiti) drawn by a Spanish cartographer. As shown, the island is divided between the two ruling empires of Spain and France.

Jean Baptiste Point du Sable was born around 1745 in the village of St. Marc on the island of St. Domingue—the area is now known as Haiti. His mother was a free black slave who is believed to have been killed in Haiti when du Sable was ten. His father was a white French mariner who owned a fleet of ships. Upon the death of his mother, who was killed during a Spanish raid on his village in 1755, the young du Sable had to swim out to sea where he found refuge aboard one of his father's ships.

Du Sable's father eventually sailed him to France to receive a proper education, and it was there that du Sable developed a love of language. He learned to speak English and Spanish in addition to his native tongue:

French. In France, he also became enamored with fine art and culture, and he later acquired several valuable works of art. In time, du Sable began sailing as a seaman for his father. On one of his voyages, du Sable traveled from St. Domingue (Haiti) to the French colony of New Orleans. On route, the ship was damaged, but du Sable abandoned it before it sank. Together with a childhood friend named Jacques Phillippe Clamorgan, an injured du Sable made it to the mainland but without the paperwork that identified him as a free person. To make matters worse, New Orleans had been seized by the Spanish, who would certainly view du Sable as not only a man worthy of imprisonment but also enslavement.

To his relief, French Jesuits rescued and protected du Sable while he mended. Du Sable did not remain in New Orleans long. After recovering, he wisely departed the Spanish-occupied territory to explore the wild interior of the North. Du Sable's friend Jacques Clamorgan, who would later become quite wealthy himself, accompanied him. Du Sable did not traipse off into the unknown foolhardily, however. Before they embarked on their journey, the two men met with a member of the Choctaw people who was a native to the Great Lakes region. He worked for a Catholic mission, and du Sable convinced him to join the expedition north along the Mississippi River. The Choctaw man taught du Sable and Clamorgan the art of trapping animals and routine survival skills. By the next spring, the Chocktaw man introduced the two explorers to Chief Pontiac, a legendary intertribal leader of the Great Lakes who led his people against British military occupation in Pontiac's War.

Chief Pontiac grew to like, respect, and trust both men, to the point where he enlisted them to negotiate peace with neighboring tribes such as the Illinois, the Ottawa, and the Miami. Before long, du Sable, Clamorgan, and the Choc-

₁n Baptiste's Cabin

₃27 illustration of the cabin belonging to Jean Baptiste Point du
₂. It was built just north of the Chicago River near Lake Michigan in
. It is believed the cabin stood approximately where the Tribune Tow-
today. Du Sable sold his estate to Jean Baptiste La Lime in 1800, and
₁me then sold it to William Burnett, a business partner of John Kinzie.
₁e, who was thought to be the original settler of Chicago for years,
₁ht the cabin and property from Burnett in 1804 and sold it in 1828.
₁rader Antoine Ouilmette's house can be seen in the background.

taw man trekked throughout the neighboring territories and established trade with various tribes and even Europeans. By the 1770s, du Sable settled in Peoria, Illinois. He was eventually accepted as a member of the surrounding Potawatomi tribe, whose languages he learned. Du Sable's good relations with the Native Americans encouraged him to establish a farm and trading post on the northern bank of the Chicago River around 1779. While the cabin he built is usually depicted as a modest, humble structure, descriptions from the era reveal that du Sable lived more luxurious than is currently thought.

Documents from the sale of du Sable's 800-acre property in 1800 describe his cabin as spacious, and complete with a stone fireplace and a large salon with five corner rooms. The estate also enjoyed bakehouses, smokehouses, stables, living quarters for employees—mainly from the Potawatomi tribe—and a garden and orchard residing in a fenced area. And let's not forget the aforementioned collection of artwork he acquired, in addition to fine mirrors and walnut furniture. Du Sable also owned a supply station, a mill, a dairy, hogs, horses, and livestock.

During the American Revolution, du Sable was forced off his land for a time, and he established another trading post in Michigan. But following the war, du Sable returned to his Chicago estate. Du Sable married a woman from the Potawatomi tribe named Kihihawa, but he called her Catherine. Together they had a son named Jean Baptiste Point du Sable, Jr. and a daughter named Suzanne. Following the sale of his property on May 7, 1800, du Sable returned to Peoria, Illinois before relocating to St. Charles, Missouri. He died in St. Charles at his daughter's home on August 28, 1818, and was buried in a nearby Catholic cemetery. Ⓤ

The Statue of Jean Baptiste

This illustration depicts the bronze bust at 401 North Michigan Avenue on the Magnificent Mile, a commercial district adjacent to downtown Chicago. Created by Erik Blome in 2009, it was donated to the Chicago Public Art Collection by Lesley Benodin to honor the founder of the city.

Gabriel's Conspiracy
e Most Extensive Slave Uprising Plot in the American South

Banner image features an illustration of Richmond, VA in 1870. Published in *The Richmond Progress*.

If not for an unprecedented evening storm that deposited torrential rain on central Virginia at the end of August 1800, rendering the dirt roads impassable, a slave conspiracy the likes of which the South had never seen may have succeeded. An elaborate and well-coordinated conspiracy was dashed by the storm, as were the hopes of the hundreds of slaves in central Virginia who were privy to it. The man behind what was perhaps the most extensive plot of slave uprising in the history of the American South was an educated blacksmith named Gabriel, an enslaved black man who was owned by Thomas Prosser. Gabriel, who stood 6 feet 3 inches tall, was an imposing figure, with muscles that developed as a result of his trade.

His plan was also thwarted by two anxious slaves who divulged the entire plot to their master. Arrests were quickly made and a trial took place throughout Virginia. Another Prosser slave, Ben Woolfolk, was pardoned on the condition that he testify against the other conspirators. From his account, we learn all the intricate details of the proposed insurrection. Weeks earlier, on a July Sunday, Gabriel was in the country north of Richmond, Virginia when he joined a group of slaves who were relaxing on a bridge that overlooked a brook. Many of them were field hands enjoying the day off.

It was an ideal recreation spot for slaves because they could listen to outdoor preaching while they ate and drank and enjoyed the company of one another. Woolfolk revealed that immediately after the sermon, Gabriel desired "to bring on the business as soon as possible," thus the plan was discussed then and there. Gabriel claimed to have something on the order of ten thousand men on his side. In quoting *The Great Stain* by historian Noel Rae:

 he had one thousand in Richmond, about six hundred in Caroline, and nearly five hundred at the coal pits, besides others at different places, and that he expected the poor white people would also join him."

The plan, according to the witness for the prosecution, was for the core group to assemble at the briery spot near the brook they frequented on Sundays. One hundred men were to remain on the bridge and Gabriel was to lead another hundred toward town to Gregory's tavern where they were to take up the arms stored there. Another fifty men were to go to a riverside warehouse district in Richmond called Rocketts to set it ablaze. This would act as a distraction to draw a crowd from the upper part of town. While the fire was being put out, Gabriel and his men were to seize the Capitol, along with all the arms from the Virginia State Armory, and put to great slaughter all who were gathered at Rocketts.

A co-conspirator named Sam Bird was to use free papers to make his way to the Catawbas natives and convince them to join the fight against the oppressive whites. Governor James Monroe was to be taken hostage as a bargaining chip that would assure the freedom of Virginia slaves. And the consensus was that all of the whites were to be massacred save for the Quakers, Methodists, and Frenchmen, who were all in favor of black liberation. Poor white women with no slaves were also to be spared. In the end, the treasury was to be drained and its spoils divided among the insurrectionists.

But no one accounted for the torrents of rain that poured down as though the heavens had forcefully repudiated the plans of the slaves. The conspirators could not gather because of it. Just before the storm, two Meadow Farm slaves named Tom and Pharaoh had already grown anxious and carried the plot to their master, Mosby Sheppard. Gabriel and many others were apprehended, and trials were held in Richmond, Norfolk, Petersburg, and other surrounding counties. They were tried in courts of oyer and terminer, which were Latin terms for courts of criminal jurisdiction based on a 1692 statute that allowed testimony to be heard by five justices with no jury present. And appeals could only be made to the governor. Noel Rae wrote of the trial:

> seven men were condemned on a Thursday and hanged on Friday. All in all, about thirty-five were condemned to death, and many others banished. Gabriel himself escaped but was soon captured, tried, convicted, and hanged. [Governor] Monroe interviewed him before his execution but got little out of him. 'He seemed to have made up his mind to die, and to have resolved to say but little on the subject of the conspiracy.' "

Battle of Yorktown

General Cornwallis surrenders to General George Washington after the siege of Yorktown.

The spirit of resistance that empowered Gabriel is the very spirit that fueled other leaders of slave revolts throughout history. The desire for freedom and liberty was a powerful driving force for all those who were ready to risk death to secure both. White colonists exhibited the same spirit in their rebellion against Great Britain during the War of Independence a quarter-century earlier.

But it was unfathomable to think that blacks could find it in them to rise against the oppressive powers that kept them chained and shackled both physically and mentally within a system that regarded them as nothing more than chattel.

In the wake of the uprising, Virginia law and broader American politics were altered. This was seen most vividly in the new Virginia laws that further restricted slaves and free blacks, as well as the presidential campaign that unfolded that year. But more recently, Gabriel's plot has been viewed in a better light by Virginia officials. Over two decades ago, a small park in Henrico County was dedicated to Gabriel and two historical markers were erected near the sites where he and his co-conspirators were to gather at the Brook Bridge and where he was made leader of the insurrection. In 2002, a resolution was passed by Richmond officials to mark the 202nd anniversary of Gabriel's planned uprising. Five years later, Governor Tim Kaine pardoned Gabriel and his co-conspirators, stating:

> the end of slavery and the furtherance of equality for all people—has prevailed in the light of history." **U**

Gabriel

Proposed depiction of the leader of one of the greatest uprisings in the history of the American South.

Horace King
The Respected Bridge Architect and Builder in the Deep Sou

Banner image features a portrait of bridge builder Horace King.

At a time when a small percentage of slaves could read or write, one slave from the Deep South defied the odds by becoming a well-regarded bridge builder in the region. Horace King is noted for constructing impressive lattice truss bridges made of heavy timber between the 1830s and 1880s, which required precise knowledge of how trusses carried stress loads. His bridges spanned many important rivers in Georgia, northeast Mississippi, and Alabama. King started his bridge-building career as a slave, partnering with his master John Godwin. But by 1860, King was among the wealthy free blacks of Alabama who traveled without restriction. King became so respected and sought after by white Southerners that, over time, several towns falsely credited him as the architect of bridges and buildings he likely did not build.

But by 1860, King was among the wealthy free blacks of Alabama who traveled without restriction.

Horace King was born a slave in Chesterfield District, South Carolina on September 8, 1807. He was of mixed African, European, and Catawba heritage. Upon his master's death, he was purchased by contractor John Godwin of Cheraw, South Carolina in 1830. King learned to read and write at an early age, and he acquired carpentry and mechanics skills as a teen. He remained near his place of birth until the age of 23 and was introduced to bridge construction around age 17.

In 1824, a bridge architect named Ithiel Town traveled to Cheraw, South Carolina to aid construction efforts on a bridge project at the Pee Dee River—Godwin had been contracted to work on the same bridge. Four years later, the span was replaced. While records do not indicate whether or not King worked on the bridge, Ithiel Town's signature lattice trusses figured prominently in Horace King's bridge architecture going forward, so he had taken special note.

In 1837, John Godwin, perhaps in an attempt to protect his valuable investment from the hands of creditors, transferred ownership of Horace King to his wife Ann Godwin and her uncle William Carney Wright of Montgomery, who was also her financial guardian. Ann and William allowed King to marry a free black woman named Frances Gould Thomas in

1839. This was unusual for a slave master, but King was no ordinary slave. Since Frances was free, this guaranteed the freedom of children produced from her union with King, of which there were five.

In the years that followed his marriage to Frances, King continued to construct bridges in partnership with his former master, John Godwin. Godwin negotiated the proposed fees with investors, while King oversaw design and construction. While the investors made their money by collecting bridge tolls, revenue derived from the building projects was likely split between Godwin and King, and by 1946, King was able to purchase his freedom. His working relationship with Godwin, however, remained the same until Godwin died in 1859.

Four years earlier, King established a different partnership with two men for the Moore's Bridge project, which was constructed over the Chattahoochee River. Instead of taking his usual fee, King opted for stock this time and essentially owned a thirty-three percent stake in the bridge. King moved his family to Moore's Bridge around 1858, and following his master's death, he was able to travel quite freely throughout the South via railroad to oversee various construction projects. As a show of respect, King erected a monument over his master's grave.

Frances and the children collected tolls on Moore's Bridge and farmed the land there. The tolls served as steady income for the family while King continued to design and build bridges and buildings in Georgia and Alabama. This dynamic lasted until July 1864, three years into the Civil War. That month, a Union cavalry commanded by General George Stoneman rode in and burned Moore's Bridge down. Frances died a few months later and King married another woman, Sarah Jane McManus, the next summer.

The Union army burned many of King's bridges during the Civil War, and while his sympathies were not with the South, he was contracted to build various projects for the Confederacy. They also forced him to block certain waterways in Georgia and Alabama to prevent Union forces from entering. The end of the war provid-

Columbus City Bridge

Horace King built this bridge for the third time in 1865. Union troops burned the previous bridge down at the same site half a year earlier.

Floating Spiral Staircase

After the Alabama state capitol burned, officials hired Horace King (along with many other architects and builders) to design and construct a new capitol building. In addition to leading the shoring (or propping) construction project for the capitol dome, Horace created a beautiful three-story floating staircase at the heart of the capitol building employing a cantilever technique used on bridges. Photo courtesy of the Library of Congress.

ed many opportunities for builders, and King benefitted from a bevy of projects assigned to him, such as a 32,000-square-foot cotton warehouse in Columbus, reconstruction of the Columbus City Bridge, three other bridges, two factories, an Alabama courthouse, and several other items.

At the dawn of the Reconstruction era, King ran for public office and was elected as a state legislator in Alabama. He successfully ran for re-election once and then withdrew from public life. He moved his family to LaGrange, Georgia shortly after and redoubled his bridge-building efforts. His construction interests expanded to include businesses and schools. In the 1870s, King began handing over construction oversight to his five children, and they established the King Brothers Bridge Company.

Horace King's health deteriorated in the 1880s, and on May 28, 1885, while in LaGrange, he died at the age of 77. King has since received various posthumous honors, and he is fondly remembered throughout the South and beyond for his creative contributions. **U**

Horace King in His Younger Days

Following his death, obituaries praising him appeared in major Georgia newspapers, which was rare for black Americans living in the South in the 1880s.

Benjamin "Pap" Singleton
Leader of the Great Exodus

Banner image features Benjamin "Pap" Singleton with a Kansas township backdrop.

B orn into slavery in 1809, Benjamin "Pap" Singleton, unable to bear the wicked institution any longer, escaped after a few decades and did so several times despite being captured and sold repeatedly. After each escape, he returned to his native Nashville. In a final bid to avoid recapture, he made his way north, to Windsor, Ontario, shortly after relocating to Detroit, Michigan, where he opened a boardinghouse for other escaped slaves.

Following the Civil War, Benjamin returned to Tennessee once more and dedicated himself to help improve the lives of other blacks. Late in the decade, he began organizing efforts to purchase tracts of Tennessee farmland for his people. But his efforts were thwarted by bigoted white landowners who raised land prices far beyond market value. Together with that, lingering racial animosities prevailed in the Upper South.

For Benjamin, Kansas, which held the promise of freedom and offered new economic opportunities and education for blacks, held greater appeal. Kansas drew many blacks west in its territorial days, during its statehood, and well into the twentieth century. While slavery existed in Kansas in Benjamin's day, slave holdings in the state were small in comparison to those in the south. More than that, black migrants routinely secured work in Kansas as hired laborers and escaped slaves passed through the state as part of the

Taking Flight to Kansas

When the federal government's Reconstruction program ended in 1877, many blacks left the South in search of a better life. This engraving depicts several Exodusters en route to Kansas as they fled from another enemy: yellow fever.

network that was the Underground Railroad. While Kansas experienced a violent pre-Civil War history that saw clashes over slavery, it emerged as an ideal free state in the eyes of blacks. They considered the state a kind of promised land, hence the name it was eventually given: "New Canaan." Unlike Tennessee, land in Kansas was also reasonably priced.

Benjamin became a zealous promoter and, together with an associate named Columbus Johnson, eventually founded the Edgefield Real Estate and Homestead Association. Using printed leaflets and handouts, Benjamin started to announce the splendors of life in Kansas, and the benefits blacks would derive by moving to the state and living in independent black communities. Through the Edgefield Real Estate and Homestead Association, Benjamin held public meetings in Nashville that functioned like church revivals. In those meetings, information about the proposed black Kansas colonies was shared and the overall migration venture was heavily promoted.

On the strength of his promotion efforts, Benjamin successfully guided hundreds of settlers from the Upper South to Baxter Springs in Cherokee County, Kansas in

Ho for Kansas!

Brethren, Friends, & Fellow Citizens:

I feel thankful to inform you that the

REAL ESTATE

AND

Homestead Association,

Will Leave Here the

15th of April, 1878,

In pursuit of Homes in the Southwestern Lands of America, at Transportation Rates, cheaper than ever was known before.

For full information inquire of

Benj. Singleton, better known as old Pap,

NO. 5 NORTH FRONT STREET.

Beware of Speculators and Adventurers, as it is a dangerous thing to fall in their hands.

Nashville, Tenn., March 18, 1878.

"Ho for Kansas!" Advertisement

This flyer for the Nashville-based Real Estate and Homestead Association announced their departure for Kansas on April 15, 1878.

1877. The following year, he led an even larger group to Dunlop County, Kansas. These were two newly created colony towns in Kansas that joined one that formed a few months earlier called Nicodemus, which was settled by a separate group of black migrants from Tennessee. The three early settlements represented the first of several migrations from the south, as waves of blacks eventually fled the post-Reconstruction states following the withdrawal of federal troops. This shift saw a return of racial oppression through Jim Crow laws that enforced segregation. And terrorism was unleashed on blacks via the Ku Klux Klan, which rose to power in the south.

This spate of activities spurred a more desperate and economically disadvantaged set of blacks to migrate west than those seen in Benjamin's two early groups, who were considered moderately wealthy. The new migrants were known as "Exodusters," and by 1879—the year of the "Great Exodus"—around 50,000 blacks sought freedom by fleeing to Kansas, Illinois, Missouri, and Indiana. Benjamin "Pap" Singleton, therefore, is considered a leader of that Great Exodus, though he harbored mixed feelings about the tens of thousands who followed in his footsteps. While Benjamin's was an organized and well-funded effort, the Exodusters descended on Kansas in a haphazard affair and threatened the stability of the established colonies which could hardly support a large influx of newcomers seeing the established farms operated on thin profit margins.

The colonies were well established, however, and in light of that, Benjamin moved onto a new venture in aid of his people. In the early 1890s, he moved to a black section of Topeka, Kansas called "Tennessee Town" due to the large number of black people who had moved there from the state. While there, he organized a party called the United Colored Links, which had ties to the Greenbacks, a labor party of midwestern whites who sought reforms that favored agrarian interests. Benjamin, through his United Colored Links, sought to protect black laborers and drum up support for the establishment of black industrial businesses. While it attracted members during a summer convention, the lack of capital in the black community doomed the venture, forcing Benjamin to move on to yet other endeavors.

In the 1880s, Benjamin took up the black nationalism cause. In 1883, his Chief League was set up to encourage and aid blacks in emigrating to the Mediterranean island of Cyprus. When that failed, Benjamin then encouraged blacks to return to Africa, and he established the United Trans-Atlantic Society to do so. By 1887, the pan-African movement fizzled, and the aging Benjamin retired from his self-imposed mission to aid blacks. Benjamin "Pap" Singleton died in Missouri on February 17, 1900, at the ripe old age of 91. **U**

Aerial View of Kansas City, Missouri (1869)

Many newly-freed blacks traveling by steamboat arrived in river cities like Kansas City before making their way to desired settlements.

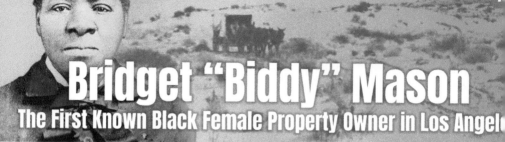

Bridget "Biddy" Mason
The First Known Black Female Property Owner in Los Angeles

Banner image features a composite portrait of Bridget "Biddy" Mason and the Mormon Pioneer trail.

Bridget "Biddy" Mason was brought to Los Angeles, California in 1851 as a slave. When she died, she was a free woman and the city's wealthiest, having risen to the level of a black real estate tycoon worth multiple millions when accounting for inflation. She is noted as one of the first prominent Los Angeles landowners of the late-nineteenth century, and the founder of the First African Methodist Episcopal Church, which was established in 1872 in the city of Los Angeles.

Biddy was born into slavery on August 15, 1818—likely in Hancock County, Georgia. She was named Bridget but had no surname for many years. The nickname "Biddy" was bestowed by her first master. The record of her childhood has been lost, but it is believed she was sold to slaveholders in Mississippi as a baby. At age 18, Biddy was presented as a gift to a young newlywed couple in Mississippi, Robert and Rebecca Smith, whom she served as a nurse and midwife. While she lived on the Smith farm she cared for Rebecca, who was often sick, as well as her children. Biddy also worked the fields and tended to the livestock.

Around 1848, Robert Smith, who had converted to the Mormon faith and was lured by the promise of a New Zion on Earth, set out with his family and slaves on a long trek due West. He met up with a wagon caravan of Mormons along the way, and together, they wound a path through the

Westward Migration
Mormon pioneers entering the Salt Lake Valley through Emigration Canyon in 1847.

rugged terrain of several states. Biddy, meanwhile—who had given birth to three daughters on the Smith farm—walked most of the way with her newborn, Harriet, strapped to her back. Her other two daughters, Ellen and Anne, were aged 10 and 4, Smith being the father of the two youngest ones, Anne and Harriet. Biddy continued to serve as a midwife to humans and animals alike along the 1700-mile trek, and she also set up camp, cooked, herded cattle, tended to the six Smith children in addition to her own, and broke camp when it was time to move on.

Following the seven-month journey, Robert Smith settled in the Salt Lake Valley—which was still a Mexican territory. There he resided for about three years before the desire for better land and prospects drew him to San Bernardino in a new U.S. state called California. He was warned by Mormon leader Brigham Young to avoid California, which was an anti-slavery state, but Smith forged ahead undaunted.

Biddy and her children were taken to San Bernardino, where Robert Smith settled after securing land along the Santa Ana River. The Mormons established a trading post and missionary church in San Bernardino while Smith entered the cattle business and did well for a time. But Biddy was making friends with black Southern Californians who had been freed from slavery, such as a couple named Charles and Elizabeth Rowan. They advised her to seek freedom on the grounds of California law. She also met wealthy black residents Robert and Winnie Owens. Robert owned a livery stable, and his son, Charles, began courting Biddy's eldest daughter, Ellen.

She was a free woman and the city's wealthiest, having risen to the level of a black real estate tycoon.

What Biddy did not know was, under California law, she and her children were technically free the moment they crossed the border into the state. The California constitution stated:

> Neither slavery nor involuntary servitude unless for the punishment of crimes shall ever be tolerated in this state."

Regardless of this, Biddy continued to serve Robert Smith, who lied to her about the conditions of her freedom. The death of Smith's wife caused him to become disillusioned with the Mormon church, and he grew fearful of losing his slaves in California. In 1855, Smith took Biddy and her daughters, and his other slaves to Santa Monica Canyon, where they camped until he could make his way to the slave state of Texas. Elizabeth Rowan, who mistrusted Smith, contacted Los Angeles County Sheriff Frank Dewitt, alerting him to the danger Biddy and the other slaves were in. The Sheriff, accompanied by a posse, rode into Smith's camp and served him with a writ of habeas corpus, thereby summoning him to appear in court for:

Biddy, who by law was not allowed to testify against a white person, was given the privilege by U.S. District Judge Benjamin Hayes. With that, Biddy challenged Robert Smith in court for her freedom during a trial that was rife with bribery, attempted kidnapping, and threats of harm on the part of Smith and his supporters. But in the end, Judge Hayes ruled that:

All of the said persons of color are entitled to their freedom and are free forever."

As a result of that January 1856 ruling, 14 slaves won their freedom. Biddy and her daughters were finally allowed to live a life removed from slavery. They moved in with the Owens family, but shortly after, Anne, Biddy's middle child, died—most likely of smallpox. But mourning eventually gave way to celebration when Charles and Ellen wed. Biddy was also able to use her skills when she was hired as a midwife and nurse by a white Southerner named Dr. John Strother Griffin. She was paid $2.50 per day, which was much higher than the average black woman was paid at the time. Biddy was able to save a considerable amount of money while delivering hundreds of babies and nursing patients during a smallpox epidemic in the mid-1860s.

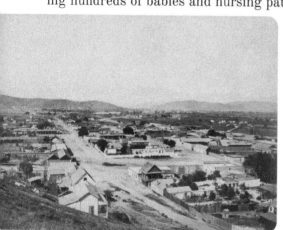

Los Angeles, California

Seen from Fort Hill, this is the city as it existed in 1877. City officials started to grade the streets shortly after California became a state in 1850.

With her savings, Biddy purchased land for $250 at 331 Spring Street, which is now in the heart of downtown Los Angeles. She built a small wood-frame house there and established the First AME Church in her new home. She also welcomed the needy. Los Angeles was not yet what it is today. In Biddy's time, it existed as a dusty town with about 2,000 citizens, of which only 20 or so were black. Biddy came to be known by all of them, from the mayor down, as "Aunt Biddy."

Biddy eventually set up her own midwifery business, but both her former employer, Dr. Griffin, and her brother-in-law, Robert Owens, had invested in real estate. They encouraged Biddy to do the same. After buying the Spring Street land, Biddy invested in other properties. Biddy proved to be a savvy businesswoman, and her investments began to pay off. She bought land cheap, held onto the parcels for a few years, then sold the same parcels for considerable sums of money. Her Spring Street home was soon accompanied by boarding houses, shops, and other businesses, as Los Angeles transitioned from a dusty rural town to a bustling city.

By the mid-1880s, Biddy was living in an apartment on the second floor of a brick building she built, while the bottom half was a commercial rental. She helped members of her extended family purchase land around the city as well. Biddy also became a philanthropist as her wealth increased. She started a daycare, visited prisoners with baskets of food, donated to charities, and covered the salary of the AME minister as well as annual church taxes. When disaster struck in 1884, and homes were flooded by the Los Angeles River during a storm, Biddy kept an account at the Spring Street grocer for all affected homeowners, be they black or white. She was loved and appreciated by the citizens of Los Angeles, but after she died in 1891 at age 73, her legacy was largely forgotten and she was buried in an unmarked grave in Boyle Heights. This oversight was corrected nearly a century later by the mayor and officials of the AME church she founded, and her accomplishments and established legacy are now being honored by the current generation. **U**

Aunt Biddy the Midwife

Book cover illustration of *With Open Hands*, by author Jeri Chase Ferris and artist Ralph L. Ramstad. The book is named for a motto Biddy often stated: "The open hand is blessed, for it gives in abundance, even as it receives." Her black medicine bag is said to have held her medical instruments and the freedom papers she received from U.S. District Judge Benjamin Hayes.

Stephen Bishop
The First Great American Cave Explorer

Banner image features a nineteenth-century engraving that depicts Stephen Bishop.

Kentucky's Mammoth Cave is considered more than just a cave to many. It includes deep river valleys, rolling hills, and diverse plant and animal life. All of this qualifies it as a UNESCO World Heritage Site and International Biosphere Reserve. But the cave itself—the longest known cave system in the world—is the feature that transformed Mammoth into a must-see destination that draws over two million visitors each year. One man is responsible for mapping the limestone labyrinth's most popular spots and making them accessible to tourists: a mixed-race slave named Stephen Bishop.

A Mammoth Experience

Visitors on a tour of Mammoth Cave enjoy sweeping views of the cave's structures and formations. Photo courtesy of the National Park Service.

Stephen was born into slavery in 1821, but very little is known of his early years. He was believed to be the biological son of Lowry Bishop, a white farmer who was his previous owner. In the spring of 1838, when Stephen was 17, his new owner, a lawyer named Franklin Gorin, brought him and two other slaves to a cave he had recently purchased for $5,000. Intending to turn the cave into a tourism site, Gorin's slaves would serve as guides. The cave, which contained five levels stacked one on top of the other, featured underground rivers, interconnected caverns, pits, underwater springs, and passageways that stretched for 412 miles.

Archaeologists have discovered that early Native Americans explored the first three levels of the cave system perhaps as far back as 4,000 years ago. As white settlers made their way west following several expeditions, the cave was rediscovered in the 1790s. In another two decades, during the War of 1812, the cave was mined for potassium nitrate (or saltpeter) for use in gunpowder. Early tourism efforts began in 1816, and even in 1838, when Gorin took possession of the cave, only eight miles of the entire system had been explored.

The superintendent who once ran the mining operation took Stephen on a tour of some of those eight miles and he received instruction on the then-current methods of being a tour guide. Thus he began guiding tourists, but he also ventured off on his own to explore passages and areas that were yet unknown. Stephen is now regarded as one of the bravest spelunkers who ever existed because his explorations were extremely dangerous at the time.

The cave is much different than it was in Stephen's day. Electricity flows through the cave system now, and sediment, debris, excess plant growth, and rubble have all been removed. Stephen had to contend with all of that. He navigated the cave with merely a rope and a lantern, which could have gone out at any moment, leaving him stranded in perfect darkness many miles within the cave's complex. Despite the danger, Stephen managed to make several wonderful discoveries by opening up unseen sections of the cave to exploration and tourism. Yet, some of the cave's branches he discovered beyond the hole of darkness known as bottomless pit were not found again until fairly recently, through the use of modern equipment and tools.

Stephen was sold to a new master the next year, in October of 1839, along with Mammoth Cave. The new slave owner was Dr. John Croghan, nephew of William Clark, co-leader of the Lewis and Clark Expedition. When Croghan discovered Stephen's knowledge of the cave system, he invited Stephen to his Locust Grove estate for two weeks in 1842 and had him draw a map of the cave's underground passages and rooms from memory (see map below). In a rare turn for that era, when the map was published two years later, Stephen received full credit. His map, which featured 10 miles of the cave (including the portions he discovered and explored) was in use for the next forty years. The map was as accurate as was possible for

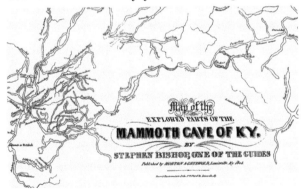

the time, absent the use of an instrumental survey, but he went to great lengths to represent the relative lengths and dimensions. He even indicated water using cross shading like modern cave cartographers do today.

Stephen named many of the areas of the cave he discovered, and those catchy names have endured: Fat Man's Misery—the narrow, winding ancient riverbed—Echo Rivers, River Styx, and Great Relief Hall. Being self-educated (he even knew a little Latin and Greek) and possessing a knowledge of geology allowed Stephen to become intimately familiar with Mammoth Cave. That familiarity, together with his colorful personality, made him a great tour guide, and he was loved by the rich, white tourists whom he guided through miles of passages for hours. It was Stephen himself—about whom articles and books were written and circulated throughout the world—who attracted visitors to that rural estate to encounter both the brave man and the mysterious cave.

Stephen also trained his eventual successors, famed slaves Mat Bransford and Nick Bransford—no relation—who Gorin leased for $100 a year. The signatures of these two guides, made from candle smoke, can still be seen throughout the cave. The two Bransfords made discoveries of their own which they infused in their tours. As it happens, descendants of Mat Bransford took up the reins and became popular tour guides of Mammoth Cave as well.

Crossing the River Styx

In this nineteenth-century wood engraving, visitors paddle one of the cave's most famous rivers.

While at Locust Grove, Stephen met and married Charlotte, another enslaved worker. She came to live with him near Mammoth Cave and worked at the hotel on the property. Stephen's enslaver, Dr. John Croghan, died in 1849 from tuberculosis. Per his will, the 28 slaves he held were to be free seven years past the time of his death. Stephen and his wife were included in that list. They were emancipated in 1856, and a year later, the two sold 112 acres of land near Mammoth Cave they had acquired from their earnings. In another few months, Stephen's cause of death is unknown.

Twenty years after Stephen was buried in an unmarked grave by his wife, a Pittsburgh, Pennsylvania visitor promised to send her a new tombstone. A few years later, the stone was indeed purchased by that visitor, millionaire James Mellon. But the tombstone was once intended for a dead Union soldier. Mellon simply had the soldier's name chiseled off and replaced with the inscription: "Stephen Bishop, First Guide & Explorer of the Mammoth Cave." Stephen was only 37 years old when he died in 1857, yet Mellow listed his date of death as June 15, 1859. And while Stephen was never enlisted in the U.S. military, the symbol at the top of the tombstone depicting downward-pointing swords is usually engraved on war memorials to honor soldiers who fought and died in battle. ∪

Mary Ann Shadd
The First Black Female Publisher of a Newspaper

Banner image features a portrait of Mary Ann Shadd.

Mary Ann Shadd was a writer, educator, abolitionist, and the second black woman in America to earn a law degree after Charlotte E. Ray. But Mary was the first black female publisher of a newspaper in both the United States and Canada. She also strongly advocated for the abolition of slavery, and she believed in equal rights for all. With the passage of the Fugitive Slave Act of 1850, which aimed to return escaped slaves back into bondage in the South, Mary's family moved to Canada. It was there that she launched her historic weekly newspaper devoted to anti-slavery measures titled the *Provincial Freeman*. Mary tirelessly promoted her anti-slavery ideas through her works, including educational booklets she wrote. They highlighted the advantages blacks would experience by settling in Canada.

Mary Ann Camberton Shadd was born in Wilmington, Delaware, on October 9, 1823. Delaware was a slave state, but her parents— Abraham Doras Shadd and Harriet Burton Parnell—were free. Her parents were active abolitionists who used their home as a "station" (or safe house) on the Underground Railroad. Her father also worked for William Lloyd Garrison's abolitionist newspaper, *The Liberator*, and was one of the first black Canadians elected to public office. Mary, the eldest of 13 children, moved with her family to West Chester, Pennsylvania in 1833, and there she attended a boarding school run by Quakers since it was illegal to teach black children in Delaware. Following her education, Mary opened a school for black children in 1840 and taught in Pennsylvania, New York, and New Jersey.

A Stamp on History

Canadian postage stamp featuring Abraham Doras Shadd.

Slavery was abolished in Britain the year Mary and her family moved to Pennsylvania, and since Canada was part of the British Empire, slavery became outlawed there as well. Canada, in effect, transformed into a national haven where escaped slaves could secure legal refuge. When it passed on September 18, 1850, the second Fugitive Slave Act caused slavery to extend well into the free Northern states.

While refugees from the slave South could be recaptured and returned to a life of enslavement via the new law, many free blacks were illegally seized and sold into slavery without recourse as well. Canada, therefore, beckoned the Shadd family (and up to 20,000 other black Americans) to migrate north. But after Mary established her weekly newspaper, the *Provincial Freeman*, she often returned to the U.S. to gather information for new articles, many of which she wrote.

Free blacks were illegally seized and sold into slavery without recourse.

Mary also resumed teaching while in Canada, this time focusing her efforts on fugitive slaves. Her school, while dedicated to blacks, was racially integrated. Public education was not open to black students at the time, so only those who could afford the tuition attended. The school received needed support from the American Missionary Association, a nondenominational society whose aim was to provide educational opportunities for minorities in the United States. Mary was strongly opposed to segregated schools for black students. After engaging in a public debate with Henry and Mary Bibb—two prominent individuals in favor of segregation—she lost funding from the American Missionary Association due to the dispute.

Mary married Thomas F. Cary, a Toronto barber, in 1856. The couple had a daughter, who they named Sarah Elizabeth. When Cary died sometime in 1860, Mary was pregnant with their son, Linton. The paper she had started was co-edited by Samuel Ringgold Ward, an escaped slave and popular public speaker living in Toronto. By 1860, it stopped printing due to financial difficulties. Three years later, around the start of the Civil War, Mary returned to the U.S. to aid the North. She settled in Indiana and became a recruiting officer for the Union Army at the urging of Martin Delany. In her role, she encouraged blacks to enlist and fight against the Confederacy, which was perfectly in line with her early anti-slavery efforts.

After the Civil War, Mary resumed her teaching career, first in Wilmington, Delaware, then Washington, D.C., where she lived with her daughter and taught public schools for fifteen years. Ever the enterprising woman, Mary later attended the School of Law at Howard University and graduated with a law degree when she was 60 years old. Around that time, she fought for women's suffrage alongside stalwarts like Susan B. Anthony and Elizabeth Cady Stanton after joining the National Woman Suffrage Association. Mary died on June 5, 1893, in Washington, D.C. The cause was stomach cancer. She was buried at Columbian Harmony Cemetery until all of its graves moved to National Harmony Memorial Park in Landover, Maryland, around 1960. Mary Ann Shadd Cary has since received several honors in Canada. Among them is a designation as a Person of National Historic Significance. **U**

Freedom's Journal
The First Black-Owned and Operated Newspaper in U.S. History

Banner image features Samuel E. Cornish and John B. Russwurm, founders of *Freedom's Journal*.

Until the early nineteenth century, the mention of blacks in white mainstream newspapers was often connected with a crime. That state of affairs was challenged on March 16, 1827, when a four-page, four-column weekly newspaper was established. And this was no ordinary paper. *Freedom's Journal*, as it was called, was the first black-owned and operated newspaper in U.S. history. The year it came into being, slavery was officially abolished in the state of New York.

New York City

View of South Street, from Maiden Lane in New York City, ca. 1827. Painted by British artist William James Bennett. Image courtesy of the Metropolitan Museum of Art.

This change allowed a group of free black New York residents to give voice to a reform movement that was opposed to the dominant racist views of the white press. Out of this group, a Presbyterian minister named Samuel E. Cornish was the senior editor and John Brown Russwurm, an early black college graduate, served as the junior editor. *Freedom's Journal* was circulated across 11 states, as well as the District of Columbia, Canada, Haiti, and Europe.

Samuel Cornish resigned as editor six months after the paper's launch, leaving John Russwurm as sole editor. They had fallen out over the issue of black colonization, an agenda Russwurm was bent on pushing and which Cornish was against. Among the topics covered in *Freedom's Jour-*

nal were: current events, world news, anti-slavery and anti-lynching editorials, broad injustices, biographies of important black figures, and a record of marriages, births, and deaths in the black community of New York City. *Freedom's Journal* also ran ads that cost between 25 and 75 cents.

Until the early nineteenth century, the mention of blacks in white mainstream newspapers was often connected with a crime. That state of affairs was challenged on March 16, 1827, when a four-page, four-column weekly newspaper was established.

The paper lasted from 1827 to 1829, spanning 103 issues in two volumes. As a result of *Freedom's Journal*, more than 300,000 black Northerners had access to knowledge of world events and current issues that directly impacted blacks. The biographies of notable black figures acted as a means of racial upliftment. Readers were lavished with features such as the one on the affluent shipping magnate Paul Cuffee, a black Quaker who employed black workers and advocated for the colonization and emigration of blacks to Africa.

Aside from the editors and staff, the paper dispatched sometimes dozens of hired agents to handle subscriptions, which was $3 per year. One such agent was a man named David Walker, who created quite a stir when, in 1829, he penned the first of four antislavery articles that called for slave resistance. In it Walker argued:

> It is no more harm for you to kill the man who is trying to kill you than it is for you to take a drink of water."

As a hired agent, Walker personally distributed the paper containing his appeal throughout the South, where it was largely banned. With Samuel Cornish's departure in 1827, *Freedom's Journal* adopted a softer tone and became increasingly pro-colonization, as its sole editor John Russwurm, in support of a predominantly white organization called the American Colonization Society, repeatedly argued for the repatriation of blacks to the continent of Africa. Readers largely rejected this view and, as a result, sales suffered. Russwurm published the last issue of *Freedom's Journal* on March 28, 1829.

Holding firm to his beliefs on repatriation, he moved to Liberia and launched another paper called the *Liberia Herald*. Samuel Cornish made a brief return to the newspaper business in May of 1829 as well, when he resurrected *Freedom's Journal* under the title *The Rights of All*. That publication lasted for several months and soon disappeared. While *Freedom's Journal* only ran for two years, its influence was far-reaching, and it acted as a model for no less than 40 black abolitionist newspapers that arose throughout the U.S. after its closure and before the Civil War. **U**

Sarah J. Garnet

First Black Female Principal of a New York City Public School

Banner image features portrait of Sarah J. Garnet from the 1911 *Brooklyn Daily Eagle* obituary.

Sarah Jane Smith Thompson Garnet was the first black female principal in the New York public school system. She also co-founded and led the Equal Suffrage League in Brooklyn sometime in the late 1880s, which was the first-ever suffrage club for black women, preceding the Alpha Suffrage Club founded by Ida B. Wells. The Equal Suffrage League was a small organization of well-to-do black women who first met in Sarah's home and the seamstress shop she owned on what is now Dekalb Avenue, and then at the Carlton Avenue YMCA in Fort Greene as the club became popular. Black suffragists of the day advocated not only for women's voting rights but also for justice and equality for the entire community of black people. To them, voting was an integral component in the fight for civil rights, proper education, economic freedom, and racial impartiality.

Sarah was born Sarah Jane Smith in Brooklyn on July 31, 1831. Her parents were Sylvanus and Ann Smith, prosperous farmers who owned land in Queens County, which, at that time, was part of Long Island. Sarah was the first of 11 children, all of whom eventually received a good education. Sarah's primary lessons were lovingly taught by her first teacher, her grandmother Sylvia Hobbs. Her father Sylvanus was a founder of Weeksville, an early all-black community in Brooklyn where Sarah was raised. Sylvanus was also one of the few black men with the right to vote since he paid a $250 property requirement that came with the privilege. This qualification was removed for white men in 1820, thus making the act a racial injustice. Weeksville and other black settlements in Brooklyn were established to circumvent the discrimination and allow coveted voting rights to

Weeksville, Brooklyn

Photo courtesy of Susan De Vries,

extend to blacks who held land.

At fourteen years of age, Sarah joined the American workforce as a teacher's assistant at a salary of $20 per year. She continued with her studies by attending several normal schools (institutes that trained future teachers) in Queens County. In 1854 she became a teacher at the segregated African Free School in Williamsburg, Brooklyn. The school was started by members of the New York Manumission Society that included John Jay and Alexander Hamilton. Sarah's hard work and dedication to pedagogy was recognized and, on April 30, 1863, she was named the first black principal in the New York public school system. She became the principal of Grammar School Number 4 and Public School Number 80, which she oversaw until her retirement in 1900, 55 years after she began her teaching career.

Sarah married twice, first in the 1850s, and again in the late 1870s. She married an Episcopal minister named James Thompson at a Brooklyn church. After he died sometime in the 1860s, she remained a lifelong Episcopalian. She kept the name Thompson, but some sources record her married name as Tompkins. Around 1879, Sarah then married a Presbyterian minister and abolitionist named Henry Highland Garnet. His death in 1882 left Sarah a widow until she died in 1911.

Before retiring, Sarah co-founded the Equal Suffrage League with her famous younger sister, Susan Maria Smith McKinney Steward, the first black female physician in New York State and the third in the country. Sarah was also named superintendent of the Suffrage Department of the National Association of Colored Women (NACW), which later absorbed her suffrage club. Although she enjoyed a lasting career as an educator and administrator, Sarah J. Garnet was overshadowed by her sister Susan McKinley Steward in both life and death. Both were buried in the historic Green-Wood Cemetery in Brooklyn, yet Sarah's gray headstone, small and unassuming, sits in the shadow of Susan's grand tombstone, which is inscribed with the title "doctor," and marked with an engraved fleur-de-lis (French for "lily flower"). U

Rev. Henry Highland Garnet

Photo taken by George Rockwood in New York City.

Mary Fields

The First Black Woman to Carry Mail for the U.S. Post Office

Banner image features Mary Fields against the beautiful Montana landscape.

Though born a slave, Mary Fields enjoyed freedom in Cascade, Montana, a pioneer community where she developed a reputation for being a tough, ill-tempered, gun-toting, black female who could hold her own with the rowdiest white men of the era. Also known as Black Mary and Stagecoach Mary, she braved the unforgiving Montana winters and fearlessly protected the stagecoach from bandits and predatory animals in her quest to deliver mail via wagon for the United States Post Office Department. She was only the second woman and the first black female contracted to do so.

Mary Fields was born into slavery in Hickman County, Tennessee sometime in 1832. Her place of birth remains a mystery and nothing is known of her early years. In the time before the Civil War, she was owned by a family known as the Warners, but she received her freedom as a result of the war. Mary left the Warner family and worked as a chambermaid and laundress on steamboats that chugged along the Mississippi River. Around this time, she made the acquaintance of Judge Edmund Dunne and took a position as a household staff member of the Dunne family.

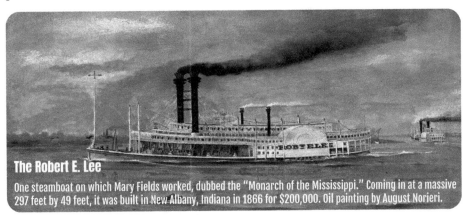

The Robert E. Lee

One steamboat on which Mary Fields worked, dubbed the "Monarch of the Mississippi." Coming in at a massive 297 feet by 49 feet, it was built in New Albany, Indiana in 1866 for $200,000. Oil painting by August Norieri.

One of Judge Dunne's younger sisters was Sarah Theresa Dunne, who established a lifelong friendship with Mary. As a child, Sarah was accidentally poisoned, and she developed asthma and several other health issues that plagued her throughout her life. Sarah and her older sister, Mary, were students at an Ursuline boarding school, and years later, in 1861, Sarah entered the Ursuline convent in Toledo, Ohio, and took her vows three years later. She adopted the name Mary Amadeus and became mother superior of the convent in 1872. In 1884, Mother Mary Amadeus founded a new mission school for girls at the St. Peter's Mission near Cascade, Montana, a small railroad town in Central Montana. The next year, Mother Mary Amadeus, who was not fit for the isolated pioneer life, caught pneumonia and soon found herself on the brink of death.

When Mary Fields heard her friend was gravely ill, she left Ohio and headed west to offer her services. With her old friend attending to her, Mother Mary Amadeus made a full recovery, and she asked Mary Fields to stay on and work at the convent. Mary happily agreed to it. She acted as foreman during the repair of the mission's buildings then fell into a routine of washing laundry, managing the kitchen, buying needed supplies, tending to the garden, and maintaining the grounds. But Mary Fields, who stood six feet tall and weighed some two hundred pounds, proved to be rougher around the edges than the nuns or the bishop liked. She brazenly wore men's jackets and boots and exhibited an unsparing temper with little provocation. And she didn't hold back from cursing, smoking, or drinking in front of the keepers of the convent.

When an argument between Mary and a hired male worker threatened gunplay, with the two drawing loaded weapons on each other, her employment ended. The bishop ordered her to leave. Mary settled in nearby Cascade, Montana, where she opened a restaurant that failed from the start. A series of odd jobs followed, and in 1895, after hitching up a team of six horses faster than any other applicant, Mary secured a contract with the United States Post Office Department to deliver mail as a coach driver. She was awarded two four-year contracts on the star route, which is a

thinly populated route in a rural area served by a private mail carrier. In this way, she carried mail in the rocky terrain of the Cascade County region for eight years straight without missing a day. In time, she became a legend in the role and earned the nickname Stagecoach Mary on the strength of her success in delivering mail on a regular schedule.

After her second contract expired, she retired as a mail carrier at the age of 71 and settled in Cascade by opening a laundry business and babysitting children in her home. Mary died in Cascade in 1914. She was also buried there by neighbors in the Hillside Cemetery, with a simple wooden crucifix marking the grave. **U**

Mary Fields

After settling down to a quieter life in Cascade.

Cathay Williams
The Only Known Female Buffalo Soldier

Banner image features Cathay Williams, as depicted on a lithograph of a painting by Frank Spivey.

Cathay Williams was a black female who enlisted in the United States Army by posing as a man and using the pseudonym William Cathay. She made history by becoming the first black American woman to join the United States Armed Forces. An act of Congress established the first all-black military units collectively dubbed the "Buffalo Soldiers"—a nickname given out of respect by Native Americans. Women were not allowed to enlist as soldiers in the Army at the time, and Cathay was considered contraband since she was a captured slave. But she saw an opportunity to achieve a level of independence as a young single female and happily volunteered her service to the Army in 1866.

Cathay Williams was born in Independence, Missouri in 1844. Her father was a free man but her mother was still a slave, which meant that Cathay was also a slave. She was raised on the Johnson plantation near Jefferson City, Missouri, where she became a house slave to William Johnson in adolescence and served him until he died. When Union forces besieged and occupied Jefferson City in 1861 at the outset of the Civil War, captured slaves—who were officially labeled contraband—were forced into military service as support staff. They became cooks, nurses, and laundry workers.

The 13th Union Army Corps took Cathay along to Little Rock, Arkansas when she was 17. Cathay became an Army cook and laundress, for which she eventually received both freedom and pay. In this capacity, she traveled with her infantry throughout the South and saw several Civil War

General Philip Sheridan
During his time in the Union Army.

battles, such as the one at Pea Ridge in March 1862. Cathay proved so capable in her service as a supporting staff member she was sent to Washington to work for General Philip Sheridan and his men. During her time with General Sheridan, Cathay witnessed his Shenandoah Valley raids in 1864.

After the war, Cathay's services were no longer needed, but as an unmarried black woman in the post-Civil War South, job opportunities were virtually nonexistent. She also faced a high level of discrimination and inequality. One sure way to secure financial freedom and gain access to healthcare, proper education, and other benefits during this period was to join the Army. Cathay planned to sidestep Army regulations and pose as William Cathay to enlist. On November 15, 1866, Cathay, aged 22, stood before a recruiting officer in her new guise and said she was an experienced cook. She was described as 5 feet 9 inches, and her hair, eyes, and complexion were listed as black.

Though Cathay was examined by an Army surgeon, medical examinations were not as thorough as they are now, so she was quickly determined fit for active duty. Cathay was assigned to Company A of the 38th U.S. Colored Infantry Regiment at Jefferson Barracks near St. Louis, Missouri. She was thereafter stationed with her infantry in New Mexico Territory, and they patrolled the transcontinental railroads which were under construction at the time. Cathay was trained as a soldier. She learned to march, handle muskets, and other military disciplines. While in the West, the 38th Infantry took up the fight against Native Americans during the Indian Wars. They were ordered to protect pioneers bound for California as they made the dangerous trek through Cooke's Canyon. In the January 2, 1876 issue of the *St. Louis Times*, Cathay told her life story. In it she revealed:

> The regiment I joined wore the Zouave uniform and only two persons, a cousin and a particular friend, members of the regiment, knew that I was a woman. They never 'blowed' on me. They were partly the cause of my joining the Army. Another reason was I wanted to make my own living and not be dependent on relations or friends."

Cathay also spoke of the health problems she faced during her enlistment. Shortly after joining the Army, she contracted smallpox and was hospitalized. After recovering, she joined Company A in the West. But her health issues resumed in New Mexico and she was sent to the hospital on several occasions. In the summer of 1868, Cathay was admitted to Fort Bayard hospital, where she was diagnosed with neuralgia—a broad term used for acute pain brought on by nerves. This hospital visit, Cathay admitted, exposed her secret. She told the *St. Louis Times*:

Fort Bayard Medical Hospital

The fort was established in August 1866 by Co B of the 125th U.S. Colored Infantry on Apache

> "The post surgeon found out I was a woman and I got my discharge. The men all wanted to get rid of me after they found out I was a woman. Some of them acted real bad to me."

She was honorably discharged at Fort Bayard in October 1868, on the grounds of disability, as well as physical and mental feebleness. It was also stated that these conditions existed before Cathay's enlistment. Years later, in 1891, that particular point was raised to deny her application for an Army pension. Her service in the Army was also invalidated when it was discovered that Private William Cathay was a woman.

After being discharged, Cathay found work as a cook for an Army colonel at Fort Union, New Mexico. She held that position from 1869 to 1870 and then relocated to Pueblo, Colorado, where she was briefly employed as a laundry worker. She finally settled in Trinidad, Colorado in 1872. She earned money working as a laundress and nurse until her health issues resurfaced. Cathay spent over a year in the hospital beginning in 1890, and emerged penniless, hence her attempt to file for a pension based on her two years of military service. Cathay's trail runs cold following this point, and without a means to support herself, it is doubtful she lived to see the twentieth century. She is thought to have died sometime between 1892 and 1900 since her name disappeared from Census rolls after 1900. ⑪

Other Female Impostors

When Cathay Williams applied for a disability pension, she expected to receive payment. She was not the first female who disguised herself as a man to join the military, after all. Deborah Sampson did it in 1816 when she joined Patriot forces during the American Revolution. Mary Ludwig Hays McCauley (also known as Molly Pitcher) allegedly fought in the Battle of Monmouth during the same war disguised as a man. Anna Maria Lane is a third woman of the American Revolution. Unlike Cathay, all three were granted pensions for serving in the war as men. And while Cathay was black, they were white.

Around 400 women posed as male soldiers during the Civil War, many enlisting alongside their brothers, fiancés, or husbands. And just as the situation with Cathay, their secrets became known when they sought treatment at a hospital. After Cathay, other black women also disguised themselves, like the one pictured here. Some mistake her for Cathay.

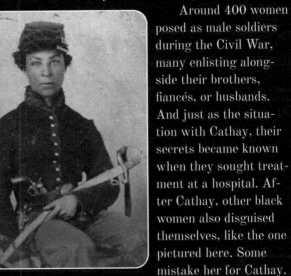

Lewis Howard Latimer
The Black Inventor Who Improved the Light Bulb

Banner image features Lewis Howard Latimer at work as a Draftsman. Bulb image courtesy of Burak K./Pexels.

Though hardly a household name, black inventor Lewis Howard Latimer influenced the evolution of the marvel that is electric lighting, which the world enjoys today. Having worked closely with two giants in the field of invention—Thomas Edison and Alexander Graham Bell—Lewis used his acquired skill and knowledge to help patent both the light bulb and telephone. He also worked as a draftsman and inventor.

Lewis Howard Latimer was born in Chelsea, Massachusetts on September 4, 1848, but he was raised in Boston. He and his three older siblings were the children of escaped slaves named George and Rebecca Latimer. Six years before Lewis was born, his parents fled slavery in Virginia, but his father George was captured in Boston and tried by his owner. During his trial, he was defended by Frederick Douglass and William Lloyd Garrison, two leading abolitionists of the day.

With the help of a minister, George Latimer purchased his freedom, but fear of the repercussions from the Supreme Court's ruling in the Dred Scott case—which protected the rights of slave owners—caused the elder Latimer to flee with his family again, this time to Chelsea, Massachusetts, where Lewis was born. Fear of being reenslaved consumed George Latimer, which caused him to abandon the family altogether, and he disappeared not long after. The Latimer children were split up, with the boys sent to live on a farm, and the girls sent to stay with a friend of the family.

With his father gone, Lewis helped support the family by finding work, and on September 16, 1863, at the age of 15, he enlisted in the Union Navy by convincing recruiters he was three years older. Lewis served on the military steamer the USS *Massasoit* as a landsman, the lowest rank reserved for recruits with no sea experience. After nearly two years of service, he was honorably discharged. Shortly after that, Lewis landed a job as an office boy at Crosby, Halsted, and Gould, a patent firm in Boston.

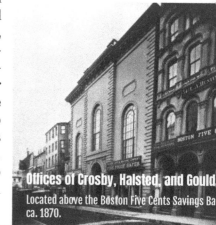

Offices of Crosby, Halsted, and Gould
Located above the Boston Five Cents Savings Ba
ca. 1870.

It was there that Lewis immersed himself in the world of mechanical drawing and was so dedicated to the craft he used his own money to purchase drafting instruments and books. In his diary, Lewis admits to looking . . .

over the draftsman's shoulder, to see how he used his instruments."

This aided him because he was soon tasked with assisting draftsmen with their drawings. And by age eighteen, the partners of the firm promoted Lewis to lead draftsman after realizing the skills and abilities he possessed, which had been self-taught. He held the position for ten years. Lewis also designed several inventions, among them a railroad car water closet (or toilet system) that was an improvement on the existing ones, and a precursor of the air conditioning unit.

On November 10, 1873, before he arrived at his first invention, Lewis married Mary Wilson, with whom he had two daughters, Jeanette and Louise. Then in 1876, Alexander Graham Bell personally hired Lewis—by then a master draftsman—to create drawings for the patent application related to Bell's telephone. A few years later, Lewis entered the competitive electrical field when he moved to Bridgeport, Connecticut, and worked for the U.S. Electric Lighting Company in Brooklyn, New York. The company's owner was Hiram Maxim, who was Thomas Edison's rival. His time at Maxim's company allowed Lewis to acquire additional technical and legal knowledge that would establish him as an expert patent witness in years to come. While at Electric Lighting, Lewis successfully improved incandescent lamps by producing a carbon filament that was more durable than the popular variety in wide use. The invention positioned Hiram Maxim's company as a viable competitor to Edison's.

Recognizing Lewis Latimer's great promise, Thomas Edison hired him away from Hiram Maxim and eventually promoted him to lead patent investigator. Later in his career, Lewis made history again by becoming a founding member—and the only black one—of a group of 100 Edison employees known as the Edison Pioneers. They were an impressive collection of chemists, engineers, draftsmen, lawyers, industrialists, inventors, and entrepreneurs. They were Edison's elite inner circle, and Lewis Howard Latimer sat comfortably among them.

Apart from his career as an engineer, draftsman, inventor, patent consultant, and expert patent witness, Lewis was also a writer, poet, playwright, and flutist. He retired in 1924 with his legacy firmly intact. In 2006, he was inducted into the National Inventors Hall of Fame. U

Thomas "Blind Tom" Wiggins
A Born Slave Turned Piano Virtuoso

Banner image features Thomas "Blind Tom" Wiggins seated at his piano.

Aslave named Charity struggled to deliver her baby on a Georgia plantation in the spring of 1849. She was 48 years old, and the child born to her on May 25 was a son, who she named Thomas. When Charity discovered that Thomas was blind, it deeply concerned her, and she feared repercussions from her master, Wiley Jones. Jones did despise the child and refused to feed him, but Charity did what she could to preserve his life. Several months later, her family, which totaled five, was sold to pay off some of the debt incurred by her master. Charity pleaded with General James Neil Bethune, who was in the market for slaves, to buy her entire family at auction. Little did Bethune know that by agreeing to do so, he would acquire a tidy fortune.

Charity Wiggins

Mother of Thomas.

Bethune, a lawyer from Columbus, Georgia, who had become a general during the Creek War of 1832, purchased Charity, her husband Domingo, and Thomas and his two older siblings. The General changed Thomas's name to Thomas Greene Bethune. There were seven children in the Bethune family who were all musically inclined. Some sang while others played the piano, and during their practice sessions, young Thomas stood by and listened with rapt attention. Thomas's blindness was not the only thing that made him different. From a young age, he had difficulty walking or expressing himself and therefore communicated with unfamiliar gestures. He was often pugnacious, and some nights he suffered seizures. Thomas could also recall phrases and details he heard in conversation. Today he is thought to have been autistic.

Listening was something Thomas did well. He spent hours listening to everything around him: wind blowing, rain falling on the roof, pots and pans clanging in the kitchen, and many other sounds of life. But the sonatas and minuets the Bethune children rehearsed commanded his attention most. He drew on his talent for memorizing phrases when, at only two years of age, he recited songs in perfect melody he heard sung once by Bethune's son. Thomas snuck into the parlor at one point, sat at the piano, and played a song he memorized while listening to one of Bethune's daughters. After a moment, the family rushed in to see who it was. When General Bethune heard Thomas play, he quickly realized he had a piano virtuoso on his hands. Thomas would go on to play piano in a career that spanned almost fifty years.

Thomas and General Bethune

Taken before 1884.

Bethune arranged for Thomas to have formal piano lessons, but it wasn't long before the student's abilities exceeded those of the teacher. Bethune saw his opportunity to create an income stream. The General hired various musicians to play pieces for Thomas to memorize, and before long, the piano prodigy had a complete concert repertoire. At age eight, Thomas gave his first concert to a sellout audience in Columbus, Georgia, which received rave reviews. In 1859, when Thomas was nine or ten years old, General Bethune contracted with a traveling showman named Perry Oliver to feature Thomas for three years, for which Bethune received $15,000. Oliver billed Thomas as "Blind Tom" and kept him to a grueling schedule of four performances a day. In the first year alone, the concerts brought in $100,000 (or more than $3 million when accounting for inflation). That figure ranks him among the highest-paid performers of his day.

Thomas astounded audiences with his gift for mimicry. He imitated his favorite sounds during performances, such as bird calls, the sound of wind, rain, and even locomotives. Thomas often treated his audiences to a rare feat during each performance. He played two songs simultaneously in separate keys with each hand and sang a third without missing a note. Each show included a challenge. Thomas invited a musician from the audience to play a composition he had never heard. Thomas would not only inform the audience of each note played, but he also performed the piece from memory shortly after.

While he could memorize and recite a fifteen-minute long discourse without understanding a single sentence, Thomas could speak a total of about 100 words on his own. Dr. Edward Seguin, a physician who introduced the psychological method, studied the young savant and published his findings in 1866. Despite this limitation, Thomas's repertoire included more than seven thousand classical pieces and popular songs. He could sing French and German songs after hearing them once. Astonishing abilities such as these brought him before the President of the United States, James Buchanan, at age eleven. They allowed him to perform freely on the stages of opera houses and concert halls throughout Europe and America during celebrated tours. But his mental disorder also left him vulnerable to exploitation by the Bethune family.

Shortly after the Civil War ended, Bethune arranged for Thomas to remain in his service for another five years. He had his parents (Charity and Domingo) sign a contract to that effect, which entitled them to a modest house and $500 a year. Thomas received only $240 each year and ten percent of the profits from the performances. Bethune kept the bulk. In July 1870, when the contract between Bethune and Thomas's parents was about to expire, John Bethune—General Bethune's son—went before a judge to prove Thomas incompetent and, therefore, incapable of managing his affairs. The judge appointed John as his new guardian. The Bethune family enjoyed this new arrangement.

Thomas's performances continued to earn hundreds of thousands of dollars throughout the years, and John Bethune lived extravagantly as a result. John moved Thomas to a Greenwich Village boarding house in New York City in 1875. A train accident claimed John's life nine years later, and Thomas's guardianship was vied for in court by several Bethune family members for three years. John's estranged wife, Eliza, was the victor, but she still needed to obtain the legal consent of Charity Wiggins. Eliza convinced Charity to make her Thomas's guardian, and with the deed done, Eliza, who remarried, moved Thomas to Hoboken, New Jersey, and supported herself with his earnings.

Financial problems still plagued Eliza, however, which kept her in court fighting lawsuits. Fearing the income she exploited from Thomas would be seized in court, she locked him away in a New York apartment and even barred Charity from seeing him. Charity expressed her regret to a newspaper reporter before she died in 1902, saying:

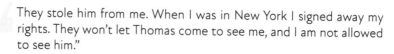

> They stole him from me. When I was in New York I signed away my rights. They won't let Thomas come to see me, and I am not allowed to see him."

After her final court battle, Eliza allowed Thomas to resume his performances, and he played a few concerts between 1904 and 1906. On June 13, 1908, while in Hoboken, New Jersey, Thomas suffered a stroke that claimed his life. He was 59. So ended the career of the man who concert promoters billed as:

> The Wonder of the World—The Marvel of the Age! The Greatest Living Musician." U

Edward Bouchet
First Black Person to Earn a PhD from an American University

Banner image features Edward Bouchet and lithograph of early Yale College campus.

Edward Bouchet made history in 1876 when he became the first black American to be named a PhD physicist. He passed his education on to other blacks through a career as a science teacher at a time when black students had few avenues to such learning. But Edward was also restricted from advancing in his career, which, had he been white, held the promise of a tenured professorship at a prestigious university.

Edward Alexander Bouchet was born September 15, 1852, in New Haven, Connecticut. His father, William Bouchet, had won freedom from slavery. As an unskilled laborer, he obtained work as a janitor at Yale University (then known as Yale College). Edward's mother was Susan Cooley Bouchet, a housewife who raised Edward and the three sisters who preceded him in birth. As a sideline, she also laundered clothes for Yale students.

Yale University's Connecticut Hall

Located on the school's Old Brick Row, Connecticut Hall is the oldest building from the colonial period and the only one that survives. It served as a dormitory for 200 years.

From a young age, the Bouchet children were instilled with Christian principles and were churchgoing. With anti-slavery sentiments running high in that period, they were also active abolitionists at a local level, and their parents stressed the importance of getting a decent education.

Despite their encouragement, however, William and Susan never dreamed that their young son, faced with the racial prejudices still prevalent in society, would one day attend Yale.

Despite their encouragement, however, William and Susan never dreamed that their young son, faced with the racial prejudices still prevalent in society, would one day attend Yale. The school he attended in his youth, Artisan Street Colored School, was segregated and staffed with one teacher, Sarah Wilson, who taught 30 students primary lessons. Edward was further encouraged by Sarah to pursue a higher education before he left to attend New Haven High School for two years. In 1868, when Edward was about the age of 16, he was admitted to Hopkins Grammar School, which was a private preparatory school of prestige, whose graduates often went on to Yale. There, Edward studied the classics, learning Latin and Greek, in addition to algebra, geometry, and history. He excelled at Hopkins and graduated in 1870, first in his class. With that, he was accepted to Yale, which he entered in the fall of that year.

It has long been held that Edward Bouchet was not only the first black person to attend Yale University, but the first of his people to also graduate. Yale itself attested to that supposed fact for many years, but in 2014, new information surfaced, which throws new light on that legend. Concerning this, Connecticuthistory.org states:

> Research by several scholars and writers, including some at Yale, indicated that three men thought to be white and who preceded Bouchet at the school—Moses Simon (Class of 1809), Randall Lee Gibson (Class of 1853), and Richard Henry Green (class of 1857)—at various times appear in public records as Negro, black, and mulatto."

Whether he was the first or fourth black student to attend Yale, by all appearances he was the first to earn a doctorate degree. Thus, Edward Bouchet sits comfortably in the historical records as an important trailblazer in the field of science. Edward remained at home while he attended Yale, but his studies never suffered. He graduated in June of 1874, sixth in a class of 124. He entered a new PhD physics program at Yale after graduating. Two years later, with his graduate studies and dissertation, "Measuring Refractive Indices" behind him, Edward became the sixth person in the United States—of any ethnicity—to receive a PhD in physics. And no other black American had received a PhD in any field before him.

As qualified and educated as he was, Edward's superior abilities were not enough to sail through the tide of racial discrimination he encountered when his search for employment began. Everywhere he turned he met with failure. Every university and college he applied to rejected him. There he was, a brilliant PhD physicist, young, capable, and eager to expend his energies in furthering his field of study, Edward was forced to teach at a segregated school for blacks, the Institute for Colored Youth (ICY) in Philadelphia. If there is a bright side in his career, he was able to teach what he loved, as the school opened up a new science program he was able to lead.

Students at the Institute of Colored Youth

A Quaker philanthropist named Richard Humphreys founded the school as the African Institute in February 1837. By April of that year, the name changed to the Institute of Colored Youth. In 1902, the school moved 25 miles west of Philadelphia to a 275-acre farm owned by George Cheyney. Today the school is known as the Cheyney University of Pennsylvania.

He taught at ICY for 26 years, his tenure culminating in 1902. That is the year his school, moving in lockstep to the philosophy of Booker T. Washington, dissolved the academic platform at ICY and instituted an industrial one, thus transforming the institution into a vocational school. Edward was out of a job. The next 14 years saw him teaching or sitting as an administrator at various high schools across the country. His health declined as he aged, and he was forced into retirement in 1916, which allowed him to return to New Haven. He remained in the very home he grew up in until his death at age 66 in 1918. He died unmarried and childless. A touching obituary written by a friend of Edward's regarded him as . . .

> a man of keen sensibilities and unusual refinement. He was a prolific reader and was greatly interested in the history of his own people and of his native town."

While Edward had educated the next generation of black youth in his chosen field of science, the exclusion of blacks from higher scientific education left him as the only black PhD physicist until 1918. Over four decades after he had received his doctorate in physics, Elmer Imes rose to become the second black American to do the same. 𝐔

Rosa L. Dixon
The Influential Educator and Reformer

Banner image features Rosa L. Dixon and historic Richmond, Virginia.

Rosa L. Dixon was a noted teacher and civic leader who was a key figure in implementing and sustaining educational reforms in Virginia, which benefited blacks. After the Civil War, Dixon and her family moved to Richmond, where she attended public school and thrived academically. She later became the first black teacher hired by a Virginia school. Dissatisfied with the state of the education system and the low social status of blacks, Rosa worked toward improving their lives through various measures. She helped found the state's first teacher's association for black Americans, which she later served as president, and presided over a women's Christian union that pushed for social reform. She was also involved in other black reform organizations, suffrage groups, black schools, and anti-lynching/segregation associations.

Rosa L. Dixon was born in Amelia County, Virginia, on January 7, 1855. She was likely a slave. Her parents were Henry Dixon, a carpenter, and Augusta Anderson Hawkins Dixon, a domestic worker. After moving to Richmond, the family renewed their commitment to religion and education. Henry and Augusta joined the First African Baptist Church—the largest congregation in Richmond—and enrolled Rosa in public school. Her early teachers were northerners from the Freedmen's Bureau. The superintendent of the Freedmen's Bureau for schools in Virginia was Ralza M. Manly. He selected Rosa to attend the Richmond Colored Normal School, where she trained as a teacher after

The First African Baptist Church

As it stood in the 1860s. Black Christians were met with resistance when they sought permission to form an independent congregation due to fear of another uprising akin to the one incited by Nat Turner years earlier. In the end, the assembly received approval on the condition that whites oversee its establishment, operation, and shepherding.

showing an increased aptitude in her lessons.

Rosa performed well in her reading, English, math, and music courses while at the Normal School. She graduated second in her class but spent another year studying ancient Greek and Latin, in addition to music and teaching techniques. Rosa passed the teacher's examination in 1872, and she married a fellow teacher, James Herndon Bowser, on September 4, 1879. He was the valedictorian of her Normal School class. But James quit teaching to work as a clerk in the Richmond post office. Due to either consumption or tuberculosis, he died on April 25, 1881, less than two years after marrying Rosa. Their son, Oswald Barrington Herndon Bowser, was born in 1880. Oswald later attended Howard University and became an established physician in Richmond, where he remained for the rest of his life.

After marrying, Rosa had to end her teaching career in keeping with the times, but she taught music to students in her home following the death of her husband. She resumed her professional career in 1883 when the school board hired her to teach public school students in Navy Hill School at the primary level. Rosa continued to teach for another four decades. After a year at Navy Hill, Rosa transferred to Baker School, where she received a promotion to supervisor of teachers. Twelve years later, she was named principal teacher at a night school for black men. During this time, she also taught classes at the Jackson Ward YMCA, in the heart of the black community.

Dr. Oswald Bowser

Oswald Barrington Herndon Bowser was a First Lieutenant in the Army's emergency medical corps and a member of the NAACP. Both his son and grandson also became physicians.

Rosa's reform efforts began in earnest when she organized reading circles that allowed fellow teachers to exchange information and collaborate on new teaching strategies. Teachers gained a great deal of insight from the reading circles, and Rosa was instrumental in organizing the Virginia Teachers' Reading Circle in 1887. Renamed the Virginia State Teachers Association, it became the first professional association in Virginia to represent black teachers. For two years, from 1890 to 1892, Rosa presided as president of the new organization. That position was a stepping stone to other leadership roles in various black organizations working to improve the lives of black Americans.

In 1895, Rosa founded the Woman's League in Richmond, Virginia, and was named its first president. Beginning in 1902, Rosa also served as president of the Woman's Christian Temperance Union. She chaired black conferences and gave notable speeches in support of black causes at annual gatherings. She was also active in several woman's clubs that emerged in the late nineteenth century. Perhaps the most well-known among these clubs was the National Association of Colored Women, which saw Rosa working side by side with Mary Church Terrell, a prominent black suffragist and leader in the black community.

For fifty years, Rosa taught Sunday school classes at First African Baptist Church, which her parents joined in youth. Health issues forced her into retirement from this post as well. Rosa lived to see the first public library in Richmond dedicated to black patrons open in her honor. They named the library for her in 1925. Due to complications from diabetes, Mary died peacefully at her Richmond home on February 7, 1931. **U**

Dissatisfied with the state of the education system and the low social status of blacks, Rosa worked toward improving their lives through various measures.

Mary Church Terrell

While Mary Church Terrell was born to two former slaves, the fortunes of her parents turned and they rose to prominence, allowing her to navigate the exclusive social circles of the middle and upper classes from her youth. She was among the few who used her wealth and social status to stem the tide of racial discrimination. While we've heard of the more widely publicized suffragists of the early twentieth century, Mary Church Terrell was also instrumental in advocating for women to be given the right to vote.

Learn more by scanning the Q code using the camera on you smartphone or tablet:

Daniel Hale Williams
Founder of the First Black Hospital in the U.S.

Banner image features Dr. Daniel Hale Williams and Provident Hospital, which he founded.

Daniel Hale Williams was a black physician who did the impossible during a period that produced few men of his distinction among black Americans. He worked on the south side of Chicago as a surgeon and physician to inner-city patients for years while observing the many barriers blacks faced in the medical profession. To that end, Dr. Williams founded a black-owned interracial hospital called Provident—the first of its kind in America—and, in 1893, he performed one of the earliest successful heart surgeries in the world.

Daniel Hale Williams was born in Hollidaysburg, Pennsylvania, on January 18, 1856. He was the fifth of seven children. His father, Daniel Hale Williams II, was a mixed-race barber who inherited the business from his father before him. When Daniel Hale Williams II died, Daniel's mother, Sara Prince Williams, uprooted the family several times, moving from Hollidaysburg to Annapolis and Baltimore, Maryland. To ease the burden she had to bear alone, Sara sent Daniel to live with family friends in Janesville, Wisconsin. At age 17, Daniel followed in the footsteps of his father and grandfather and became a barber. He also played bass violin on the side, but he quickly realized that neither profession was his calling.

Daniel shifted his focus to education. He attended secondary school in Wisconsin, and by age 20, became an apprentice to the state's former surgeon general, Dr. Henry Palmer. Dr. Palmer encouraged Daniel to further his medical studies, and with his sponsorship, Daniel moved to Illinois and attended Chicago Medical College. After earning his medical degree in 1883, Dr. Daniel Hale Williams served as a surgeon at Chicago's South Side Dispensary. Since the clinic was in an integrated neighborhood, he treated both black and white patients. Dr. Williams

Dr. Henry Palmer

also taught anatomy classes at Chicago Medical College, and he was the first black medical professional hired by the City Railway Company as a private surgeon.

In 1889, Dr. Williams was appointed to the board of health by the governor of Illinois. But he was still a lone representative within the black community. Dr. Williams longed to create a hospital that could accommodate white and black doctors alike, where black women could also train as nurses. Dr. Williams spent months working to make his dream a reality. He raised funds directly within the black community and, by May 1891, Provident Hospital and Nursing Training School opened its doors. The hospital featured an integrated staff from the beginning.

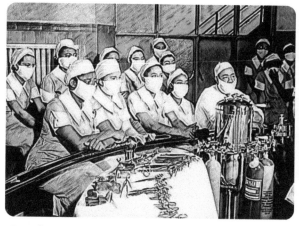

Provident Hospital Students

Here observing a doctor perform a mock operation in 1942. Adapted from a photo courtesy of the Library of Congress.

Chicago's black population finally had a dedicated facility that offered medical care with no discrimination. Provident Hospital was also the setting for the historic heart surgery performed by Dr. Williams. Doctors rarely operated on the heart in those days, and Dr. Williams would have received sharp disapproval at another facility. It all started in July 1893, when a young Chicago resident named James Cornish arrived at Provident with a stab wound in the chest. After being admitted, Cornish went into shock, and Dr. Williams surmised that the problem centered on the heart. He immediately went to work. While he performed the surgery, Dr. Williams was assisted by six doctors on staff, four white and the other two black.

As a medical pioneer, Dr. Williams did not have many previous heart surgeries on which to rely. He administered substandard anesthesia—given his limitations—and inspected the victim's chest wound in the cramped operating room. He decided that the best course of action was to access Cornish's heart through the rib cartilage. Dr. Williams began cutting. Under the chest wall, there was a rupture in Cornish's left internal mammary artery, so Dr. Williams sutured the wound.

Next, he noticed that the membranous sac around the heart, known as the pericardium, had been punctured by a knife close to the left coronary artery. As the patient bled, with no possibility of a transfusion, Dr. Williams applied a salt solution rinse to the wound and grasped its edges with forceps as the heart kept beating. Dr. Williams stitched the area as best he could and completed the surgery. After 51 days, James Cornish was allowed to leave the hospital, and he lived to tell his tale for another 20 years. Daniel Hale Williams had made history, and despite being black, the media celebrated his success.

In 1894, he moved to Washington, D.C., to serve as chief surgeon of the Freedmen's Hospital, which was a high honor. Dr. Williams worked to revitalize the hospital and decrease the mortality rate. He improved the facilities, implemented new medical procedures, and increased the staff with qualified physicians. He also introduced an ambulance service and again launched training programs for black nurses and interns. The hospital made a complete turnaround within a year. But as time passed, Washington politics and bloated medical bureaucracy grated on Dr. Williams. It is at the Freedmen's Hospital that Dr. Williams met Alice Johnson, whom he married. The newlywed couple settled in Chicago in 1898 after he resigned from his post. Dr. Williams returned to Provident Hospital and remained until 1912. The following year, he joined the American College of Surgeons as a charter member.

Freedmen's Hospital

The former Freedmen's Hospital building, seen here in 2008 as the John H. Johnson School of Communications. Photo courtesy of Wikimedia Commons.

After leaving Provident, Dr. Williams took a position as a staff surgeon at St. Luke's Hospital in Chicago. His wife Alice passed away in 1924 due to complications of Parkinson's disease. A stroke he suffered in 1926 forced him to resign. He lived in retirement for five years in Idlewild, Michigan, then an affluent resort town. While at home, Dr. Williams succumbed to another stroke on August 4, 1931. He was 75 years of age. **U**

Isaac Burns Murphy
Arguably the Greatest American Jockey

Banner image features Isaac Burns Murphy and an 1888 image of the Chicago Racetrack from *Harper's Weekly*.

Isaac Burns Murphy is considered by some to be the greatest rider in the history of American Thoroughbred horse racing. While Murphy was black, he was hardly the only black jockey of his era, because black Americans dominated the sport in that period. But Murphy was the preeminent rider among them. More recent jockeys have grabbed headlines and wowed audiences by winning prestigious races and earning multiple millions in prize money, but the stats should speak for themselves.

Touted as one of the greatest horse jockeys in living memory, Russell Avery Baze, who won 12,844 races, had a career average of over 24 percent in terms of wins. Put another way, that means almost one in every four horses he rode during a race was a winner. That stands as an industry-best when you remove Isaac Burns Murphy from the equation. Murphy himself admitted to winning 44 percent of the races he entered. Records from that time only show an average of 34.5 percent of wins, however. But many of his races were likely never entered into the chart books, which was not uncommon in those days. Regardless, a 34.5 percent winning average is yet to be matched by any other horse racing jockey, meaning Murphy set what is perhaps an unachievable standard in the sport. Horse racing Hall of Fame jockey Eddie Arcaro said of Murphy:

1860s Lexington, Kentucky

" There is no chance that his record of winning will ever be surpassed."

Isaac Burns Murphy was born free in Fayette County, Kentucky on April 16, 1861, but his parents were former slaves. His father served in the Union army during the Civil War and spent his final days as a prisoner of war in the hands of the Confederate army. Following his death, Murphy's mother moved the family to Lexington, Kentucky, where he grew up. Murphy's racing career started in 1875, and he originated what came to be known as the grandstand finish, which was a thrilling charge to the finish line where he rode upright after pacing himself throughout the race. He was known across the nation after a major 1879 win during the Travers Stakes in Saratoga Springs, New York.

Murphy was the first to win the Kentucky Derby three times, having competed in eleven, and he was also the first to win consecutive Derbies—1890 and 1891. He made history by winning the Kentucky Derby, the Kentucky Oaks, and the Clark Handicap in the same year—1884, and he was the first person of any ethnicity elected to horse racing's Hall of Fame. Murphy also developed a reputation as a man of integrity. When horse bettors attempted to bribe him to lose the Kenner Stakes in 1879 he refused. Murphy's many wins positioned him as one of the highest-paid athletes of any sport played in the U.S. at the time. His earnings allowed him to both own and train horses, which required considerable sums of money.

Churchill Downs Racetrack

Located in Louisville, Kentucky, it has been the home of the Kentucky Derby and the Kentucky Oaks since 1875.

But sadly, Murphy's career started on a steady decline in the mid-1890s mainly due to objectionable habits he adopted that not only affected his health but also his weight. The timing of his downfall coincided with the period of increased racism experienced by blacks in horse racing. Their involvement with the sport decreased considerably as a result. In the years following World War I, black jockeys were largely forgotten. In a 2009 *Smithsonian Magazine* article titled, "The Kentucky Derby's Forgotten Jockeys," Lisa K. Winkler wrote:

> In the first Kentucky Derby in 1875, 13 out of 15 jockeys were black. Among the first 28 derby winners, 15 were black."

Winkler also pointed out in 2009 that when considering modern Kentucky Derby races, where thousands of fans line up to watch the celebrated event, an unusual phenomenon was witnessed in an American sport that year:

Of some 20 riders, none are African-American."

That changed in 2013 when black jockey Kevin Krigger competed in the Kentucky Derby. In 2021, another black jockey named Kendrick Carmouche rode in the prestigious event, of which the *Associated Press* reported:

Carmouche is now one of the few remaining Black jockeys in the U.S. Much like Marlon St. Julien in 2000, Patrick Husbands in 2006, and Kevin Krigger in 2013, his presence in horse racing's biggest event is a reminder of how the industry marginalized black jockeys to the point they all but disappeared from the sport."

When Isaac Murphy died of pneumonia on February 12, 1896, he was thereafter buried in an unmarked grave, despite his past fame and many hard-won successes. It was not until the late 1960s that his burial site was located by a Kentucky researcher. Murphy's body was then exhumed and reburied in a fitting burial site in the Kentucky Horse Park. Isaac Murphy's great legacy is now starting to be remembered. **U**

Isaac Burns Murphy

With his many victories, Isaac Burns Murphy became the highest-paid jockey of his day. During his peak, he enjoyed a salary of $10,000–$20,000 per year, excluding bonuses.

Ida B. Wells
The Groundbreaking Early Civil Rights Leader

Banner image features Ida B. Wells and white suffragists protesting in front of the White House.

Ida B. Wells was a prominent journalist, editor, and co-owner of two black newspapers, and she used the power of print to expose the severity of discrimination and racial inequality experienced by blacks in America. She also denounced lynchings, actively fought for women's rights, and defied the bigotry and oppressive racism of her time with every fiber of her five-foot frame.

Ida was born into slavery on July 16, 1862, in Holly Springs, Mississippi during the Civil War. Her parents were James and Lizzy Wells, both of whom belonged to the Republican Party and were active in politics during Reconstruction. Ida's father was a member of the Freedman's Aid Society, and with them, he helped start a liberal arts school for newly freed slaves called Shaw University (the name later changed to Rust College to distinguish it from the Raleigh, NC school of the same name). James Wells was one of the school's first trustees. Rust College is one of only 10 Historically Black Colleges and Universities established before 1869 that are still active.

Rust College Students
Engaged in a mechanical drawing class, circa 1902.

Ida received her early education at Rust College but was forced to drop out when she was 16. She was orphaned at that age due to a yellow fever epidemic that claimed the lives of her parents and infant brother. She later headed to a nearby school and convinced the administrator she was 18 to work as a teacher and support her five remaining siblings. But it was when she moved to Memphis with her younger sisters that her career as a journalist and civil rights activist began. Her brothers were able to secure work as apprentices to carpenters and set out on their own.

Ida continued working as a teacher in Memphis for a time while taking classes at Fisk University in Nashville to further her education. At age 21, Ida intended to travel to Nashville as usual and purchased a first-class train ticket. But she was confronted by the conductor who ordered her to move to the less accommodating area of the train designated for blacks, despite her ticket purchase. When Ida refused, the conductor attempted to drag her out of her seat by force, and so she "fastened [her] teeth on the back of his hand," as she later wrote.

Ida was awarded a $500 settlement after suing the railroad in circuit court, but the Tennessee Supreme Court later overturned the decision. It was this action that sparked the activist fervor in Ida B. Wells. Though she worked as a teacher in a segregated Memphis school, she began to write on the side. Her unsparing pen was soon criticizing the poor condition of black-only schools in the city. In 1891, she was fired for her brutal honesty.

The next year, a friend named Tom Moss, who owned a grocery store in Memphis, was lynched, along with co-owners Calvin McDowell and Will Stewart. The black-owned store, The People's Grocery, was in direct competition with the white-owned store in the neighborhood and was considered to be stealing business. The jealous white rival gathered supporters and confronted Moss and his partners on several occasions until things came to a head. While Moss and a few associates were guarding the store one night, a few whites attempted to vandalize the black grocery and sev-

The People's Grocery

A man delivering Van Buren Cigars by horse and buggy. This may be the only surviving image of the People's Grocery, located at the corner of Mississippi Blvd and Walker Avenue, an intersection known as "the curve" because the streetcar rails curved sharply here. Featured on a postcard now in the public domain.

eral of them were shot. Moss, McDowell, and Stewart were arrested and brought to jail to await trial, but an angry white mob broke the three men out and lynched them. Ida strongly denounced the racial murders in the paper and was transformed into an investigative reporter. With a loaded pistol packed, she spent two months scouring the South looking into more than 700 lynchings that had occurred in the previous decade. In her search, she uncovered the various ways black people had been murdered in the South: some drowned, some hanged, others mutilated or burned alive, and still others beaten to death or shot, all of them because their skin was a darker hue. Ida reviewed photos, interviewed eyewitnesses, and examined newspaper articles. When she needed to, she hired private investigators.

In this, Ida exemplified a great deal of courage at a time when women could not vote and were afforded few rights, and black women yet fewer. The information she gathered was poured into anti-lynching articles that figured in her broader campaign, but one editorial had gone too far in the eyes of local whites. A white mob forced its way into her newspaper office and destroyed her equipment while she was in New York. She was warned to never return south, thus began her activism in the North.

Ida continued her anti-lynching campaign in New York, writing a detailed lynching report for the *New York Age*, a paper run by former slave T. Thomas Fortune. But it wasn't all activism and reporting for Ida. In 1895, she married Ferdinand Barnett and became Ida B. Wells-Barnett. Together the couple had four children. Ida established several civil rights organizations in her day, including the National Association of Colored Women along with her friend Mary Church Terrell, and civil rights luminary Harriet Tubman. And like Mary Church Terrell, Ida was counted among the co-founders of the NAACP. She fought tirelessly for women's suffrage and lived to see the fruits of her labor (and that of many others) with the passage of the 19th Amendment in 1920, allowing women the right to vote. Ida died on March 25, 1931, in Chicago, Illinois. The cause of death was kidney disease. She was 68 years old. **U**

The Barnetts

Portrait of Ida B. Wells-Barnett and her four children: Charles, Herman, Ida Jr., and Alfreda.

Maggie Lena Walker
The First Black Female Owner of a U.S. Bank

Banner image features Maggie Lena Walker and the St. Luke Penny Savings Bank she founded.

Though born to a former slave, Maggie Lena Walker became a civic leader, being named grand secretary of the Independent Order of St. Luke (IOSL). Once a burial society, the IOSL grew into a fraternal order that offered life insurance and death benefits to its black members. White firms denied black Americans these privileges during Jim Crow. But under Maggie's leadership, the IOSL focused on the social and financial advancement of the black community.

Maggie also founded a paper called *St. Luke Herald*. It reported the ongoing efforts of the IOSL and the various issues blacks faced in America. And despite existing laws that discriminated against women and black Americans, Maggie—being both—defied them by becoming the first black woman to establish a bank in the United States. The St. Luke Penny Savings Bank, of which Maggie was president, was built in Richmond in 1903.

Elizabeth Van Lew Mansion

Educated by anti-slavery Quakers in Philadelphia, Elizabeth Van Lew (pictured right) became a Southern abolitionist. After she completed her education, she returned to Richmond, Virginia. Her father later died, and Van Lew convinced her mother to free the blacks they had enslaved. Though the state of Virginia seceded from the Union, Van Lew used her fortune to spy for Union forces and support their efforts during the Civil War.

Maggie was born Maggie Lena Draper in Richmond, Virginia, on July 15, 1864. Her mother, Elizabeth Draper, worked on a large estate owned by a white woman named Elizabeth Van Lew—she was an abolitionist and spy for Union forces during the Civil War. Maggie was born on the estate while her mother worked as an assistant cook. It was there that Elizabeth Draper met an Irish American named Eccles Cuthbert. He was Maggie's biological father. Her parents never married, and shortly after she was born, Maggie's mother married the butler of the Van Lew estate, William Mitchell. In 1870, Elizabeth gave birth to Maggie's half-brother, John Mitchell.

Maggie's stepfather, William, left the Van Lew estate to become a head waiter at Saint Charles Hotel, a prestigious establishment in Richmond. He moved the family to a small house in College Alley, not far from the Medical College of Virginia. Disaster struck in February 1876, when authorities discovered the body of William Mitchell in the James River. Police ruled his death a suicide by drowning, but his wife suspected murder. Since William was the sole provider, Elizabeth and her children sank into poverty.

Elizabeth opened a laundry business to make ends meet. Maggie helped by delivering clean laundry to white customers in the neighborhood, which she carried in a basket balanced on her head. With access to white society, Maggie witnessed firsthand the disparity that existed between her culture and theirs. For years, Maggie was impacted by how well average whites fared compared to most blacks, and she devoted a considerable amount of her life to narrowing the divide.

Though she was poor, Maggie was still able to attend new segregated schools in Richmond. She studied at the Valley School, the Navy Hill School, and Richmond Colored Normal School, which trained future teachers. While attending the Normal School, Maggie joined the Independent Order of St. Luke, the black fraternal society. She graduated from the Normal School in 1883 and began teaching students at Valley School. She did so for the next three years until she married Armstead Walker, Jr. on September 14, 1886. School policy dictated that female teachers must be unmarried. Armstead was a brick contractor for the construction and bricklaying business owned by his family.

Armstead Walker, Jr.

Maggie dedicated herself to married life as much as to her work with the IOSL over the next decade. She gave birth to three children—a son named Russell (born in 1890); another son named Armstead (born in 1893), who died seven months later; and the youngest son, Melvin (born in 1897). The couple also adopted a daughter named Polly Anderson. While adjusting to motherhood, Maggie enjoyed a steady rise up the ranks of the IOSL. In 1895, she was named grand deputy matron of the order.

During this time, she also organized a juvenile branch of the IOSL to prepare the next generation to engage in social activism. Four years after her promotion, Maggie rose to the level of grand secretary of the IOSL, the order's highest leadership position. Maggie held the post for the rest of her life. She took over leadership when the organization was near bankruptcy. But in 1901, Maggie introduced a sweeping plan to revitalize the IOSL. As she implemented each stage of her proposal, the order not only survived but also expanded its reach.

Maggie launched the newspaper *St. Luke Herald* in 1902 to inform members of local IOSL chapters of ongoing efforts and achievements. Within another year, she founded the St. Luke Penny Savings Bank, of which she presided as president until 1929. In the twenty-five years she sat as grand secretary of the IOSL, it went from a deep deficit to collecting shy of $3.5 million with nearly $100,000 in reserve funds and around 100,000 members across twenty-four states.

Maggie continued the organization's expansion by opening the St. Luke Emporium, a department store catering to black Americans. It offered affordable goods and job opportunities for black women. Maggie introduced these enterprises in her original plan, which intended to open the black community to financial independence. As a result of the penny savings bank and its success, many black families achieved homeownership in the community, and a black middle class thrived.

Four years after her promotion, Maggie rose to the level of grand secretary of the IOSL, the order's highest leadership position. Maggie held the post for the rest of her life

Maggie and the IOSL did face setbacks during this period. A new Virginia law requiring financial institutions and fraternal societies to remain separate forced the St. Luke Penny Savings Bank to become independent in 1910. A year later, the St. Luke Emporium, which was never profitable, closed its doors. Another family tragedy compounded the struggles she faced with the order. In 1915, her son Russell Walker was alarmed one night by what he thought was an intruder. He shot the person in a panic, but it turned out to be his father returning home. Russell was arrested and tried for murder after spending five months in prison, but he was proven innocent.

The incident stayed with him for years. Unable to recover from severe depression, which drove him to alcoholism, Russell Walker died on November 23, 1923. Maggie, meanwhile, developed diabetes and received a leg wound. Her deteriorating health left her in a wheelchair until the end of her life. But she remained dedicated to her work with the IOSL. Due to complications from diabetes, Maggie died on December 15, 1934, at age 70. She rests in Richmond's Evergreen Cemetery. **U**

Covert, Michigan
The American Town That Never Experienced Segregation

Banner image features schoolchildren from Covert, Michigan, posing for a group photo.

The United States integrated almost three-quarters of a century ago, yet there are still neighborhoods and towns where blacks or whites are the only resident ethnicity. That was more prevalent in the past, during periods like Jim Crow and the Civil Rights era. But since its founding, Covert, Michigan was home to whites and blacks who lived, worked, played, and interacted as relative equals for over 150 years. Jim Crow legislation created a segregated country for the most part, and anti-black sentiments that often erupted into violence forced black Americans into isolation, which led to the establishment of many all-black communities. The citizens of Covert, Michigan—whites and blacks alike—disregarded those Jim Crow laws and lived an integrated existence at a time when that was unthinkable.

The Jim Crow South

A 1940 café near the tobacco market in Durham, North Carolina. Above the doors are separate entrances marked "white" and "colored." Photo credit: Jack Delano. Courtesy of the Library of Congress.

In 1856, a rural community was formed in the wilderness of Van Buren County, Michigan. By 1866, on the heels of the Civil War, it was settled by whites and blacks with a shared radical interest: they desired to live in a town built on equality. It was illegal for black students to sit with white students in schools across the country. The township officials in Covert sidestepped that issue by neglecting to list the ethnicity of students on rolls sent to Lansing—the capital city—for state aid. In 1868, white voters in Michigan made it illegal for blacks to vote, but a gaping hole in Michigan law said nothing about blacks running for public office.

That same year, the citizens of Covert went to the ballot to elect Dawson Pompey, a black farmer near the age of 70. Born to a slave, Pompey became the first black person to hold elective office in Michigan, where he oversaw road projects. While Pompey's election was a historic first for Covert, the township voted twenty-nine other black Americans into office over the next three decades. The offices were diverse and included drain commissioner, township trustee, constable, election inspector, and Michigan's first black justice of the peace.

These elected officials oversaw an unassuming sleepy village that became a boomtown in those thirty years. Covert's logging industry was prosperous, as were its commercial fruit farms that spread out across flat fields interspersed with farmsteads and orchards. Detroit, Chicago, and other Midwestern cities benefited from Covert's collective output. Covert was not much to speak of in terms of size. At the heart of the township was a small village, also known as Covert, which boasted thirty to fifty humble abodes, a town hall, a church, two general stores, and at one time a hotel. Beyond this cluster were the bustling sawmills, around which local lumbermen lived in crude log cabins.

Farm Life

A blueberry farm in Covert, Michigan. Photo courtesy of Jeff Schuh.

Covert attracted many blacks in the ensuing decades, all of whom sought a better existence. Black Americans migrated to the township and settled it to bask in its culture of equality. The 1870 Census reveals that no black farm was smaller than 40 acres, with the collective black-owned lands in Covert carrying a value of $21,600. Dawson Pompey's land alone was worth $6,000 in 1870, while the yearly wage of the average laborer was $186. This was unprecedented.

But as idyllic as Covert sounds, all was not peaceful. There were moments of strife between whites and blacks, particularly concerning labor— in this case, logging. By and large, local whites lived in harmony with the black residents of Covert, but the logging boom attracted whites from outlying areas who sought work in the mills. They disregarded the unusual race relations that were foundational to Covert. In her book *A Stronger Kinship: One Town's Extraordinary Story of Hope and Faith*, Anna-Lisa Cox writes:

> The loggers who accompanied the local logging boom were known for their violence and lawlessness. (In the 1950s an elderly Covert resident remembered that his grandfather, who had been a logger in Covert in his youth, was missing the tops and bottoms of his ears, lost to some other man's teeth during one of the many fights he had gotten into at the logging camps.)"

But a period of boom is usually followed by one of bust. This was the case with Covert's logging industry, which had become unprofitable by 1889. The residents of Covert made an important transition from lumber production to farming. The soil on Covert's farms was sandy and damp, which was best for fruit trees and shrubs. Apples, peaches, pears, and blueberries proliferated, but peaches became the preferred fruit among them.

By the mid-twentieth century, Covert's population was on the decline. Black men and women of the younger generation abandoned the township to search for work in neighboring cities. Many of those who left the unique settlement found themselves thrust into segregated communities for the first time. But in Covert, integration continued in an unbroken line from the founding of the township.

Covert Today

The town is still nestled in the Michigan wilderness. Photo courtesy of the Delta Media Group.

Today, Covert is a sprawling thirty-five square miles, complete with dense forests and blueberry farms where close to 3,000 people live, work, and play. Covert's spirit of integration continues, as it is now home to a growing population of Hispanics or Latinos. According to the 2010 Census, they make up thirty percent of the population, overtaking blacks as the second-most populous ethnicity. **U**

Pullman Porters
Pioneers of the Black Middle Class

Banner image features a group of Pullman Porters. Photo courtesy of the Transportation Communications Union.

Before commercial air travel or the highway system that allowed passenger cars to carry people across the country, Americans traveled long distances by passenger train. After the Civil War, George M. Pullman, a white businessman from Chicago, exclusively hired thousands of black Americans from the South to work for his company. Pullman specialized in building luxury railroad sleeping cars, within which wealthy white passengers could travel in comfort while being served by Pullman's black employees. They were known as Pullman porters, a collective of underpaid, overworked blacks who bore racism while establishing a black middle class through their demanding livelihood.

George Mortimer Pullman, who was born in 1831, did not invent the sleeper car. A company known as the Cumberland

Prompt Service

In this 1952 Pullman Company advertisement, a black Pullman porter donning a white uniform stands at a passenger's door with a pocket watch in hand. The smiling passenger is dressing for the day, with the implication being: he was awakened right on time.

Valley Railroad beat him to it five years after he was born. They used a bunk car dubbed the *Chambersburg*, which featured fixed bunks at three different heights. In the years that followed, several railroad companies produced variations that proved uncomfortable to passengers. What Pullman conceived of and presented to the public was the luxury sleeper. He moved to Chicago in 1855, made a name for himself, and amassed a small fortune raising houses out of the swamp beneath the city.

In the mid-nineteenth century, railroads were expanding throughout the country and growing in popularity. In 1859, Pullman approached the Chicago, Alton and St. Louis Railroad with a plan: he wanted to convert two old passenger cars into luxury sleepers. They allowed him to do so, and Pullman's workers began retrofitting with no blueprint. In four months, the first palace cars were complete. They featured chandeliers, a Cherry wood interior, plush velvet seats, marble-top washstands, and two berths. Passengers could fold the upper berth against the wall to create more room for the lower berth. As an irresistible capper, Pullman decided to hire former slaves to service the train's upper-class passengers.

The first Pullman porters went to work in 1867, and they eventually became a ubiquitous and integral part of railroad travel. But as black porters, they existed at the bottom of the hierarchical structure. Pullman porters were to be at the beck and call of passengers, in addition to carrying their baggage, tidying the berths, and even shining shoes.

At the Beck and Call

A Pullman porter serves passengers in the dining car.

During slavery, masters forced their surnames on blacks. As a holdover from those days, there was the added indignity of Pullman porters having to answer to the name "George." A porter was either called George or "boy." George was the name of their employer, and it became standard practice to address Pullman porters as such, regardless of what their real names were. White men named George, who took offense, founded the Society for the Prevention of Calling Sleeping Car Porters George (or SPCSCPG). Membership grew to a staggering thirty-one thousand. Among their ranks were King George V of England, George Herman "Babe" Ruth, and other notable men named George.

In his book, *Rising from the Rails: Pullman Porters and the Making of the Black Middle Class*, author Larry Tye says of the degrading policy:

It stuck because it was repeated instinctively by successive generations of passengers, especially those below the Mason-Dixon Line, and by caricaturists, comedians, and newspaper columnists."

George Pullman did not object to this action. He thought it prudent to hire slaves as porters simply because they were accustomed to kowtowing to white elites. They would also work long, grueling hours for very little pay since their previous labor came with none. These racist actions aside, Pullman's company was a boon for black Americans in those days because it was difficult to obtain gainful employment elsewhere. At its peak in the 1920s, the railroads employed some 20,224 black Americans, more than any other industry. And their small wages still amounted to more than black workers earned in other fields. As demeaning a job as it was, with the average porter having to work 400 hours per month with hardly any time off, being a Pullman porter became a coveted career among blacks. It was not unheard of for three successive generations of men in a family to don the uniform.

The railroad industry enjoyed great success as decades passed, and in the mid-1890s, the American Railroad Union organized the Pullman Company workforce, save for the black porters. This deliberate exclusion forced blacks to organize themselves during the Roaring Twenties when they founded the Brotherhood of Sleeping Car Porters (BSCP) in 1925, led by social activist A. Philip Randolph. It was the first all-black union of its kind to engage in collective bargaining with a U.S. Corporation. But even with union backing, Pullman porters were still resisted by racist white Pullman Company elites for more than a decade. In 1937, after successful negotiations, working conditions finally improved. Pullman porters received better

The Pullman Porters Quartet

Entertaining a white audience during the Daily News Victory Travel fair. Pictured from left to right are Fred Butler, F.S. Balle, John Spencer, and W.H. Butler. B.T. Cornelius appears in the background.

pay and reduced monthly working hours, now limited to 240.

Pullman porters—whose work required them to be porters, chambermaids, waiters, valets, and entertainers rolled into one—earned a glowing reputation and were known for their unparalleled service. That created high demand for many former porters who transitioned to jobs in other industries. Some worked at upscale hotels or fine restaurants, while one porter—J.W. Mays—served several presidents in the White House. Mays first worked for President William McKinley in his private sleeping car before embarking on official White House duties for McKinley and eight successive presidents. A. Philip Randolph and the BSCP also influenced President Franklin D. Roosevelt to issue Executive Order 8802 in June 1941, which sought to ban discriminatory hiring practices by Federal agencies and the unions and companies aligned with the defense industry. The order also gave rise to the Fair Employment Practice Committee, whose goal was to enforce policies beneficial to blacks in this arena.

Faced with the social inequality between blacks and the wealthy white passengers they served, many Pullman porters sought to narrow the divide. They were able to save enough money to send their children and grandchildren to black colleges, from which they emerged as professionals. Mayors Tom Bradley of Los Angeles, Willie Brown of San Francisco, and Supreme Court Justice Thurgood Marshall descended from Pullman porters. The railroad industry helped grow the new black middle class in the 1940s and '50s, but the popularity of automobiles and airline travel also increased. These competing forms of transportation ate into the profit margins of the railroad industry and brought the Pullman Company (and its successors) to an end in 1981. The legacy of the Pullman porters, however, lives on. **U**

Legacy Builders
A dignified Pullman porter ready for duty.

C.R. Patterson and Sons
The First and Only Black American Car Manufacturer

Banner image features Charles Richard Patterson and a 1902 buggy. Photo courtesy of Daniel Berek/Flickr.

C.R. Patterson and Sons did the unthinkable at a time when hundreds of white-owned companies entered the crowded field of automobile manufacturing: it dared to compete as well. Unlike all the other players in this arena, C.R. Patterson and Sons was owned by black Americans. The automobile era came in the early twentieth century, upending the days of horse-drawn carriages by way of an internal combustible engine that delivered a different kind of horsepower.

Henry Ford used the moving assembly line to churn out hundreds of thousands of identical Model T cars that were sold relatively cheap, but C.R. Patterson and Sons—operating out of Greenfield, Ohio—built expensive custom vehicles for a smaller customer base, meaning only a few were produced. While C.R. Patterson and Sons manufactured under 200 automobiles

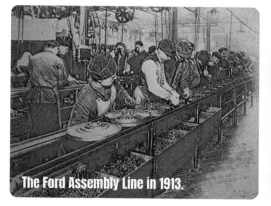

The Ford Assembly Line in 1913.

between 1915 and 1918, it positioned itself as a luxury brand that catered to blacks who could afford such luxury. But the company simply could not compete with the moving assembly line model, and there were not enough middle-class blacks who needed an expensive vehicle. Therefore, C.R. Patterson and Sons was forced out of custom automobile manufacturing. It had to adapt to stay in business.

The company made a necessary transition in the past. Its founder, Charles Richard Patterson, was born a Virginia slave in April 1833. While little is known about the period of his enslavement, he eventually gained his freedom, though conflicting records are left to us as to how he did so. Charles eventually settled in Greenfield, Ohio, which was an Underground Railroad station. He found work at the Dines and Simpson Carriage and Coach Makers Company and became a skilled blacksmith. In 1873, he formed a partnership with a white man named James P. Lowe and began building finely crafted horse-drawn carriages. After buying out his partner twenty years later, C.R. Patterson and Sons Carriage Company was established. Each year the company built surreys, phaetons, buckboards, buggies, and jitneys for medical doctors.

During its time in business, C.R. Patterson and Sons was awarded several patents, among them a trill coupling, buggy top, and vehicle dash. Charles died in 1910, and his eldest son, Frederick Douglas Patterson, assumed control of the family business. Frederick was noted as the first black football player at Ohio State University. Frederick was also appointed vice president of the National Negro Business League, which was founded by Booker T. Washington in 1900. As the new owner of C.R. Patterson and Sons, Frederick realized the need for progression. Horse-drawn carriages and buggies were fading into the past.

The company's transition was gradual, and it only repaired and restored existing horseless carriages initially. But having access to various makes and models of these new carriages allowed C.R. Patterson and Sons an opportunity to reverse-engineer the invention. Frederick advertised his auto repair services locally and in time his employees became intimately familiar with engines, drivetrains, and mechanical and electrical systems.

Frederick Douglas Patterson

Pictured with a Patterson-Greenfield automobile. Courtesy of the Historical Society of Greenfield, Ohio.

Frederick was forward-thinking. He addressed the board members by highlighting the increase of horseless carriages, which went from one vehicle for every 65,000 people in 1902 to one for every 800 in 1909. He proposed they produce a Patterson horseless carriage. In 1915, history was made when the company unveiled the Patterson-Greenfield automobile at the introductory price of $685. It came in two models: a touring car and a roadster. Later vehicles sold for as much as $850, versus Ford's $400 price point for the less sophisticated Model T.

Despite the higher cost, orders for C.R. Patterson vehicles trickled in. Between 1915 and 1918, the company produced several models, from coupes and family sedans to sporty speedsters. Among the many features advertised were a 30-horsepower Continental four-cylinder engine, a ventilated windshield with a stylish split down the center, cantilever springs, electric starting and lighting, and a full floating rear axle. In the end, the high-quality Patterson-Greenfield vehicle could not compete with the moving assembly line and the more affordable offerings from larger Detroit rivals.

The Greenfield Bus Body Company

A bus built for the school district in Greenfield, Ohio.

Between increased labor costs and the rising price of parts, supplies, and equipment, profit margins were slim for C.R. Patterson and Sons. By the early 1920s, the company—operating as the Greenfield Bus Body Company—made another transition, this time building bus and truck bodies for chassis manufactured by those Detroit rivals. The new business model worked for a time and the company was profitable until the stock market crashed and the Great Depression hit. Customers reduced bus orders after suffering financial woes, and the death of Frederick Patterson in 1932 only compounded the company's problems.

In 1938, Frederick's two sons, Frederick Jr. and Postell restructured the company again, this time naming it the Gallia Body Company and moving its headquarters to Gallipolis in southeastern Ohio. The Great Depression continued to wreak financial havoc on companies across the American landscape, and the Patterson sons could not secure investors to remain a going concern. They closed the doors on the last vestige of C.R. Patterson and Sons in 1939. No Patterson-Greenfield automobile remains in existence, but the accomplishments of a family that began in the dark bowels of slavery and rose to the elite position of automobile manufacturer should be seen as a supreme triumph. **U**

Meta Vaux Warrick Fuller
The Celebrated Sculptor of the Black Experience

Banner image features Meta and her sculptures: *The Waterboy II, Mother and Child,* and *Lazy Bones.*

Meta Vaux Warrick Fuller was a black American sculptor who expressed the black experience through her art with metaphoric pieces wrapped in symbolism. A major shift in her career came in 1921 when Meta exhibited pieces she created for a New York exposition called America's Making. She was commissioned by W.E.B. Du Bois and her contribution would figure in the "Americans of Negro Lineage" portion, but Meta was then known as the "sculptor of horrors" for her twisted bronze figures and dark themes. Du Bois, who recognized her talent and abilities, wanted something more practical and representative of black culture from the artist. Meta obliged and went on to create her most famous piece, *Ethiopia.*

Born Meta Vaux Warrick in Philadelphia, Pennsylvania on June 9, 1877, Meta grew up in a middle-class family and was allowed privileges few blacks enjoyed during the Jim Crow era. She was the youngest of three children, and was named for the Greek word, *meta,* signifying "change" or "alteration"—though the name is pronounced *mee-tah* according to her grandson, Dr. John L. Fuller, Sr. Her mother Emma (Jones) Warrick was a wig maker and hairstylist whose clientele were upper-class white women. Her father William H. Warrick was a barber and caterer. Both of her parents owned businesses and were successful, which was rare for Philadelphia blacks at the time.

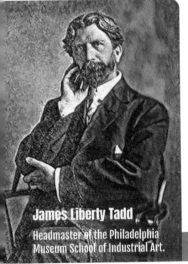

James Liberty Tadd
Headmaster of the Philadelphia
Museum School of Industrial Art.

Meta had an early education in art at home. Her older sister Blanche studied art and her father had an appreciation for sculpture and painting. Meta also furthered her art studies when she attended a segregated high school in Philadelphia in the early 1890s. She exhibited a high school project at a Chicago world's fair called the World Columbian Exhibition in 1893, and on the strength of it was awarded a scholarship to study art and design in a selective program at the Pennsylvania Museum and School of Industrial Art taught by J. Liberty Tadd. This is where she was introduced to techniques in sculpture. She earned a diploma and became a certified teacher in 1898, and made plans to sail to Paris the next year to pursue postgraduate art studies.

Meta made arrangements to stay at the American Girls' Club while overseas, but after sailing across the Atlantic, she was refused lodging by the director of the boarding house due to her skin color. Meta found other accommodations and the director of the boarding house introduced her to various art teachers. This led to Meta meeting Raphael Collin and Jean-Antonin Carles, two sculptors she studied with the next year, with a focus on drawing and anatomy.

Before leaving Paris, Meta approached Auguste Rodin—the French artist considered the founder of modern sculpture and the man behind the Thinker. Meta wanted Rodin to critique her work. When it became public knowledge that he was impressed, Meta's sculptures garnered more recognition and attention in Paris. Things changed when she returned to Philadelphia in 1903. Due to prevailing racism and gender-based discrimination, Meta was ostracized from the U.S. art scene and was unable to sell her pieces. But like many of her forebears, Meta persevered and was later rewarded.

Meta made history in 1907 when she became the first black American to receive an art commission from the U.S. government. She created the *Warrick Tableaux*, which consisted of fourteen dioramas for the Jamestown Tercentennial Exposition, celebrating three hundred years since its founding. Despite the commission and the groundbreaking work she produced, Meta was not in demand and therefore did not achieve financial success. Two years after the Jamestown exhibition, Meta married Dr. Solomon Carter Fuller, the first black person to practice psychiatry in the U.S. He was a neurologist at Massachusetts Hospital. Meta and her new husband moved to Framingham, Massachusetts, and had three sons.

Though she was expected to be a settled wife after marrying, Meta continued to pursue her art career while balancing family life. Shortly after the birth of her first son, Solomon Jr., a fire broke out at the Philadelphia warehouse that was home to Meta's art-

Ethiopia

Meta created this painted plaster maquette for *Ethiopia Awakening* in 1921. An African woman is emerging from her mummy wrappings as a representation of black people attaining full consciousness.

work, which spanned sixteen years. She began housing the collection in the warehouse after returning from Paris, but the bulk of her work was lost. Meta was so devastated she abandoned art for a few years.

W.E.B. Du Bois came calling in 1913, and he commissioned Meta to create an exhibit for the fiftieth-anniversary celebration of the Emancipation Proclamation abolishing slavery to be held in New York. The result was Meta's multi-figure piece titled *Emancipation*. Du Bois sought Meta's artistry again in 1921 for the aforementioned America's Making Exposition in New York. Her Afrocentric themes celebrated black culture, did away with dated stereotypes, and chronicled the black experience, which established her as an important member of the Harlem Renaissance.

Emancipation

Meta Vaux Warrick Fuller's multi-figure sculpture *Emancipation* on display at Harriet Tubman Square in Boston, MA. Originally created in plaster for the 1913 Emancipation Proclamation exhibit, it was cast in bronze in 1999, more than thirty years after Meta died.

In the years that followed, Meta continued to sculpt, write poetry, and paint, adding to the preserved body of work that grew to include intimate portraits of family and friends, studies, ephemera, process art pieces, and sculptures fashioned in plaster, wax, and bronze. Meta's devotion to her family was greater than her art, and when her aging husband suffered health issues and lost his sight, she became his full-time caregiver until the day he died in 1953 at the age of 81. Only then—being a woman in her late 70s—did she resume her art career.

Meta exhibited her work until 1961, the year of her last show at Howard University in Washington, D.C. Meta passed away on March 18, 1968, in Framingham, Massachusetts. She was 90 years old. Meta has since garnered posthumous recognition and support. A large majority of her art is held by private collectors, while the largest public collection can be viewed at the Danforth Art Museum at Framingham State University in Massachusetts. U

Danforth Art Museum

Home to the largest collection of works by Meta.

Nora Douglas Holt
The First Black American to Earn a Master's Degree in Mus

Banner image features Nora Holt and the Cotton Club in Harlem, ca. early 1930s.

While Nora Douglas Holt composed and sang her own music, few of her original pieces—numbering more than 200—survive. Nora was also an editor and music critic for the *Amsterdam News*, and as a socialite, she rubbed shoulders with luminaries of the Harlem Renaissance. Among her many accomplishments was co-founding the National Association of Negro Musicians in Chicago. Outside of her music career, Nora hopped through five marriages and became wealthy after the death of her fourth husband. It afforded her a great deal of independence to travel. But the party-going lifestyle she later developed was full of escapades and scandal that sullied her reputation.

Nora Holt was born Lena or Lora Douglas in Kansas City, Kansas, in 1885. Some sources list 1884 as her year of birth, but according to one close correspondent, author Carl Van Vechten, Nora was born in 1885.

Her father, Calvin Douglas, was a minister of St. Augustine's Episcopal Church. Nora's mother, Gracie Brown Douglas, steered her toward piano lessons when she was four years old. She took to the art and developed her talent by playing the church organ for several years.

The intense pull of romance drew Nora during her teens. While still in high school, she married three times. Musician

Carl Van Vechten

He was a noted American writer and photographer who frequently corresponded with Nora Douglas Holt. The two were close friends. Adapted from a photo courtesy of the Library of Congress.

Sky James became her first husband when she was 15, followed by politician Philip Scroggins two years later. Her third husband was a barber named Bruce Jones, but all three marriages were short-lived. Over a decade later, Nora married her fourth husband, the wealthy hotel owner George Holt (who she met in Chicago). She then adopted "Holt" as her married name and "Nora" as her given name. Nora also pursued an education in music by enrolling at Western University. She graduated at the top of her class.

With her bachelor's degree secured, she left Kansas for Chicago to pursue her master's at Chicago Musical College. Achieving that goal landed her in the record books, as she was the first black American to earn a music degree of that caliber in the United States. Nora's College thesis was an original work, an orchestral piece titled *Rhapsody on Negro Themes*. It is among her lost material. In 1917, she also became the first music critic for the iconic black newspaper, the *Chicago Defender*, a post she held until 1921.

Historic Holt Hotel

Though she hobnobbed with men of influence outside of her race, Nora only cavorted with men of her color. All of her husbands were also black, including George W. Holt, who was thirty years her senior. This eponymous hotel, built in Wichita Falls, Texas, in 1910, is one of the enterprises that contributed to George's wealth. The hotel is listed in the National Register of Historic Places by the United States Department of the Interior.

Two years before she left the *Chicago Defender*, Nora sought to further public interest in black musicians by co-founding the National Association of Negro Musicians with Henry Lee Grant, Duke Ellington's high school piano teacher.

After her husband died in 1921, Nora inherited his fortune. She then moved to New York and became a wild socialite during the Harlem Renaissance. During that time, several romances came and went. She eventually married her fifth husband, Joseph Ray, in 1923. Ray was a wealthy black man from Pennsylvania who was an assistant to steel magnate Charles M.

Nora Douglas Holt

Adapted portrait of Nora Douglas Holt taken by Carl Van Vechten in 1955. Courtesy of the Library of Congress.

Schwab. After the wedding, Ray established Nora in a mansion nestled in Bethlehem, Pennsylvania, but he could not keep her there. Nora was soon back in New York gallivanting with her old social circle. She aroused the jealousy of her husband by taking several illicit partners, and her marriage became embattled.

Bitter divorce proceedings lasted for several years, but when the end of her marriage finally came, the court awarded Nora tens of thousands of dollars promised to her by Ray before they wed. With that, she returned to New York and her beloved Harlem society for a time, until Europe beckoned. Nora longed to tour the continent, but before she made the journey, she arranged to have her collection of original compositions stored safely until her return. Sadly, that was the last time she or the rest of the world saw those pieces. The music went missing during her twelve years abroad, stolen by an unknown culprit. The only compositions that remain are those she published in her 1921 Chicago magazine, *Music and Poetry*.

Nora returned to her first true love, music, by playing piano and singing jazz songs in clubs across Europe and Asia. After making a splash in London and Paris—where she met American writer Gertrude Stein—Nora took her act to Shanghai. Her return to the United States came in 1938 after Japanese forces invaded China. She settled in Los Angeles, where she taught music to high school students and took part in the school board. Nora also started a successful beauty shop in the city. In the late 1930s, she also enrolled at the University of Southern California, where she continued her studies in music education.

Nora was back on the east coast in the early 1940s after being hired as an editor and music critic for the *Amsterdam News*. And in the '50s and mid-'60s, she entered the world of radio and enjoyed a new career as a musical director and producer of *Nora Holt's Concert Showcase*. The program aired weekly on the Harlem station WLIB. Indeed, Nora was as busy and active in the music world during her senior years as in her youth. She died in Los Angeles on January 25, 1974. **U**

South-View Cemetery
The Oldest Black Stockholder Corporation in the U.S.

Banner image features a view of burial plots at South-View Cemetery.

After the official end of slavery, racial discrimination did not cease, and blacks throughout the United States suffered the experience in various forms, not least segregation. In 1880s Georgia, formerly enslaved blacks in Atlanta had been pushed beyond their limit when segregation extended to the burial of their dead. Blacks living in the South wanted to retain dignity in their funerary services.

They had already been forced to erect schools and educate their children, and they built hospitals and established training schools to supply skilled medical personnel to care for the sick. Black businesses sprang up in service to various communities. As a natural extension of these developments, a fitting resting place was desired to allow for closure denied to black people living in these communities.

For Atlanta blacks, burying loved ones in this period meant entering select cemeteries via a back gate to avoid contact with whites, or worse, being restricted to services conducted in swamps, through which families would have to wade. A group of prominent black men in the community held meetings in the basement of Atlanta-based Friendship Baptist Church in 1885 for a proposed solution to the problem of lack of adequate burial. As a result of the meetings, they sought to obtain a charter from the State of Georgia via petition in February 1886. Despite racial oppression, South-View Cemetery was chartered as a joint-stock holding corporation in Atlanta on April 21, 1886, without regard to race. In her book, *South-View: An African American City of the Dead*, historian Dr. D.L. Henderson writes:

> A small number of the nation's present-day African American businesses were also founded in the late 1880s, though none were originally incorporated."

Thus, on April 21, 1886, history was made, as South-View Cemetery became the oldest black stockholder corporation in the U.S. The charter was signed by six former slaves who rose to become successful and well-respected businessmen. They were: Jacob McKinley, George W. Graham, Charles H. Morgan, John D. Render, Robert Grant, and Albert Watts, who served as the association's first treasurer, and whose family continued to administer its operation into the present day.

Nestled between downtown Atlanta and Hartsfield-Jackson Atlanta International Airport, South-View Cemetery, which started as only 25 acres, now sits in the historic Lakewood Heights neighborhood on over 100 acres of rolling hills and flat plateaus. More than 80,000 black Americans are buried on its grounds, which feature a naturalistic landscape design inspired by nineteenth-century British garden cemeteries. South-View offered more than just dignified internment of the dearly departed, however. The inviting landscape also provided a desirable green open space within a bustling city environment that was becoming increasingly busy and growing more crowded as the years passed.

While the cemetery garnered support from the beginning, over time, many more have come to see the importance of the cemetery, and the burial of notable black leaders as well as individuals who have figured prominently in black history via their struggles and contributions have only added to South-View's continuing legacy. **U**

South-View Cemetery
Another burial site, based on a photo by Nadia K. Orton.

Mound Bayou
The Historic Black Town in the Mississippi Delta

Banner image features Mound Bayou, looking north on West Main Street. Original photo credit: John Sharp.

Mound Bayou, located in the central Mississippi Delta, was once a thriving haven for thousands of black Americans during Jim Crow. Former slaves founded Mound Bayou as an all-black town in 1887, and within it sprang up dozens of black-owned businesses, including two mills, three cotton gins, a train station, a library, a few schools, and even a bank. A town of this magnitude was unheard of at the time, and the economic development it enjoyed drew the attention of many, including President Theodore Roosevelt, who called Mound Bayou "The Jewel of the Delta." Such high praise from a U.S. president was warranted, seeing Mound Bayou was a former wilderness swamp. At its height, Mound Bayou was the nation's largest black town, and the most self-sufficient one in existence.

Three cousins founded Mound Bayou: Isaiah T. Montgomery, Joshua P. T. Montgomery, and Benjamin T. Green. They had been slaves on the same property in Warren County known as Davis Bend Plantation. Their former master was Joseph Davis, older brother of Jefferson Davis, president of the Confederate states. The cousins divided up the responsibilities required in establishing a town, with Isaiah Montgomery and Benjamin Green handling the business end of things, and Joshua Montgomery dealing with the legal aspect.

Mound Bayou's Founders
Benjamin T. Green and Isaiah T. Montgomery. Courtesy of the Library of Congress.

The first order of business was securing land, and Isaiah and Benjamin accomplished that with a down payment on 840 acres in the remote rural area of Bolivar County in July 1887. Isaiah had been hired as a land agent for the Louisville, New Orleans, and Texas Railroad, as its owners were planning to build a railway line through the Mississippi Delta, which required the establishment of towns. The rail company saw newly freed blacks as an untapped source of future revenue, particularly if they were able to establish some of those towns, hence why Isaiah and others like him were hired as land agents.

After the land was purchased, Isaiah and Benjamin started to recruit settlers, from which they would draw a labor force. The land was densely overgrown with trees and undergrowth that was nearly impossible to navigate without cutting implements. Beyond that, wild animals still roamed the interior, and swamp fever eventually claimed the lives of a few settlers. More and more recruits descended on the swampland, the first waves comprising ex-slaves from Davis Bend Plantation, and then former slaves hailing from various parts of the South. Together, they did the grueling business of clearing the land. In 1907, Booker T. Washington published his account of Mound Bayou's founding, saying:

> It was not the ordinary Negro farmer who was attracted to Mound Bayou colony. It was rather an earnest and ambitious class prepared to face the hardships of this sort of pioneer work."

Under Isaiah's leadership and planning, the forest and swamp were cleared, and settlers flocked to the black colony. The founders saw their positions improve as commissions from land sales poured in. Isaiah and Benjamin established the town's single sawmill, from which everyone benefited. Then came a supply store, post office, cotton gin, school, and church. In 1898, Isaiah was appointed the town's first mayor, and other settlers filled important posts, such as marshal, aldermen, and treasurer.

Taborian Hospital

While it is closed today, Taborian Hospital served black citizens throughout the Delta region after opening in 1942.

In 1942, the black fraternal organization the International Order of Twelve Knights and Daughters of Tabor constructed a medical facility. It was the first hospital in Mound Bayou, offering forty-two beds. The hospital staff was a collection of graduates from Nashville's Meharry Medical School, and they were all black. The town, therefore, seemed to lack nothing. NPR interviewed a Mound Bayou woman named Annyce Campbell who was born in the town in 1924. She says of the town:

> You name it, we had it! We had everything but a jail, to tell you the truth!"

Annyce was born and raised when Mound Bayou enjoyed a period of prosperity. The tentacles of white supremacy were not long enough to reach into that particular black town, and Mound Bayou was even a haven from white oppression during the Civil Rights era. While blacks in other parts of the South were being dragged off and lynched, or beaten in broad daylight and attacked by police dogs, Mound Bayou residents could visit the various shops and black-owned businesses along their streets in peace. Students didn't have to worry about segregation or receiving an inferior education. Sick residents could be treated at a local hospital where every physician, nurse, and orderly looked like them. Discrimination was nonexistent in Mound Bayou, and residents drank from any water fountain they wished.

But after reaching its apex, Mound Bayou's prosperity began to decline in the latter half of the twentieth century. The town suffered economic downturns like any other community when markets spiraled. And antagonistic whites did encroach on the oasis from time to time. Internal political strife also wreaked havoc, but desegregation is what truly sealed the town's fate. When blacks were finally allowed to integrate with whites, many left their native black towns for what they hoped were better prospects. By the 1960s, Mound Bayou was struggling. Today, the town exists as a husk of its former self, with few businesses remaining, the population largely reduced, and half of the children living below the poverty line. Its residents are now fighting to regain a semblance of the glory the town enjoyed during its heyday. **U**

Bygone Days

A few fashionable Mound Bayou residents pose for their portraits during more prosperous times.

Paul Revere Williams
First Black Member of the American Institute of Architects

Banner image features Paul Revere Williams and the 1928 house he designed for banking executive Victor Rosetti.

D espite the obstacles faced by being black, Paul Revere Williams enjoyed an astonishing career as an architect. He spent close to six decades designing more than 3,000 projects, many designated for his native Los Angeles and others for various cities of the world. He came from humble beginnings yet managed to launch an architectural career in the early 1920s. Paul quickly rose to prominence in his field, even becoming the first black member of the American Institute of Architects (AIA) in 1923. He made history a second time with the same organization when, in 1957, the AIA inducted him into the College of Fellows, its highest membership honor. He was the first black architect of that distinction.

Paul Revere Williams was born in Los Angeles on February 18, 1894. He had an older brother named Chester. His parents were Chester Sr. and Lila Wright Williams, who migrated from Memphis to Los Angeles in 1893. Paul's father died from tuberculosis in 1896, and his mother suffered the same fate in 1898 when the same disease claimed her life. That left the brothers in foster care before two separate families adopted them. Paul developed an interest in art and focused on the craft in high school. While he studied architecture at a Los Angeles art institute, Paul found work as a landscape architect. At age 22, Paul enrolled at the University of California and spent three years learning architectural engineering. There, he designed his first residential buildings and later earned his degree.

A year after entering the university, Paul married Della Mae Givens in a ceremony held at the First AME Church in Los Angeles on June 27, 1917. The couple had three children, the first of which—a boy named Paul Revere Williams, Jr.—died the day he was born, on June 30, 1925. Two daughters survived. Marilyn Frances Williams was born on December 25, 1926, and Norma Lucille Williams was born on

Paul's Wife

Della Mae Givens lived to be 100 years old.

September 18, 1928.

Paul acquired his architect's license in 1921, making him the first black architect in the entire American West. He was able to begin placing his signature touch on residential homes a year later. Plans called for a new Flintridge community in the San Gabriel Valley, and developers chose Paul to design its houses. Between 1921 and 1924, Paul worked for architect John C. Austin, the designer of some of Southern California's landmark buildings, such as the Shrine Auditorium and Los Angeles City Hall. Paul established his own office and took on clients after his time with Austin ended, and while he endured racism, projects began to pour in.

Paul learned that many of his white clients objected to sitting next to a black man. So rather than draft his project designs while seated shoulder-to-shoulder with a client, he learned to draw upside down. That way, the renderings appeared right side up to the person sitting across the table from him. It became his signature practice. Paul encountered other forms of racism as well. Prevailing segregation covenants barred him from living in the white neighborhoods for which he designed homes. The Flintridge community he helped design had a land deed that restricted blacks from spending the night.

In time, big-name Hollywood clients like Cary Grant, Lucille Ball, and Desi Arnaz came knocking, and the homes Paul designed for them came to embody Southern California glamour, which the rest of the country tried to emulate. A large portion of his legacy became that of being the "architect to the stars." Frank Sinatra was one such client. When Sinatra was between marriages and looking to expand his career in film, he needed a home near the Hollywood studios. He immediately hired Paul to design it and gave him near-complete creative freedom. Sinatra had few requests. Among them: the house had to be built around a hi-fi sound system to accentuate his recorded music.

In the Zone

Frank Sinatra, Norma Williams Harvey, and Paul Revere Williams (Norma's father) hashing out designs for Sinatra's home.

To that end, Paul filled the walls of the main living area with gravel due to its acoustic properties. He also installed loudspeakers in the ceiling and other state-of-the-art equipment and controls throughout the house. After workers completed the house, it was featured on the then-popular reality television show *Person to Person*, hosted by Edward R. Murrow. Sinatra offered a walkthrough of the home, treating viewers to all of Paul's signature touches.

During the live television broadcast, Sinatra walked viewers to the dining room at the rear of the house. It opened onto a patio that overlooked Beverly Hills. Since the 1930s, Paul began reordering the standard design of homes, placing the dining room at the back and the kitchen upfront. That way, homeowners were able to enjoy their gardens, pools, or backyards as they ate. But while preparing meals at the front of the house, the street and front entrance was in view.

While Paul was instrumental in creating the California style, he operated in several architectural modes via various projects. The elegant home was far from the only structure in his oeuvre. Paul worked on projects as diverse as the Palm Springs Tennis Club, the Polo Lounge at the Beverly Hills Hotel, and federally funded housing projects like Pueblo del Rio in Los Angeles. The famous restaurateur Alex Perino also hired him to turn a Thrifti-mart market into one of the most exclusive eateries in the city. The Hollywood elite frequented Perino's in its heyday when waiters delivered food on solid silver pastry carts and trays. Today, many of the houses designed by Paul Revere Williams rarely go on the market, as their owners have come to prize them highly. 𝐔

The Beverly Hills Hotel

Paul created the aesthetics for the hotel and the Crescent Wing addition, which features the iconic Beverly Hills signature.

Beauford Delaney
Modernist Painter of the Harlem Renaissance

Banner image features Beauford Delaney regarding his 1950 pastel on paper painting "Yaddo."

I n the 1900s, around the quarter-century mark, black intellectuals and artists centered in Harlem engaged in a cultural and creative movement that attracted the world's brightest black talents. It was called the Harlem Renaissance. The year the stock market crashed, a black modernist painter who trained in Boston, Massachusetts and Knoxville, Tennessee, relocated to New York when the power and energy of the Harlem Renaissance proved too strong a draw. His name was Beauford Delaney, and his colorful, expressive paintings presented prominent black figures and New York street life in a vibrant style. Though he spent much of his career in relative obscurity, he is now considered a twentieth-century black artist of importance.

Beauford Delaney was born the eighth of ten children in Knoxville, Tennessee, on December 30, 1901. Due to inherited poverty, he was only one of four children among his siblings to survive into adulthood. His father was a barber and Methodist preacher named Samuel, and his mother was an illiterate former slave named Delia, who became a housekeeper for affluent white families in town. In light of their prominent roles in the local church, both were highly regarded members of the black community in Knoxville.

Beauford's mother, who was also a seamstress, was the one who encouraged him and his brother Joseph to foster their artistic talents. A strict, religious upbringing meant that Beauford had an active involvement in the church. Consequently, his early art mirrored the images on Sunday school cards and those found in bibles used by the family. Beauford's first commission came in his early teens, and the painting earned him a small amount of recognition.

Beauford later found work at the Post Sign Company, where he assisted in painting signposts before being trusted to create his own designs. His work gained the attention of the most successful artist in

Self-portrait of Joseph Delaney

Enoch Lloyd Branson

In 1873, Knoxville photographer T.M. Schleier snapped this photo of Branson creating a self-portrait in his studio.

Knoxville, an aging impressionist painter named Enoch Lloyd Branson, who primarily depicted early East Tennessee history and Southern politicians. Branson, a white Southerner, saw promise in Beauford's sketches. He decided to take the young artist under his wing in the early 1920s. After taking Beauford as far as he could, Branson made arrangements to send Beauford north to continue his art studies. In 1924, Beauford enrolled at a school in Boston, Massachusetts, entering the city with letters of introduction.

Before long, Beauford was rubbing shoulders with Boston's elite black activists, among them towering figures such as James Weldon Johnson, the poet, novelist and civil rights leader; Butler Roland Wilson, the trailblazing attorney and humanitarian; and William Monroe Trotter, the real estate businessman and newspaper editor. But Beauford's primary reason for being in Boston is the thing that fascinated him most: art. When not in class or working at one of his intermittent jobs, he spent his days immersing himself in art history. Beauford often visited the Isabella Stewart Gardner Museum and galleries at the Boston Museum of Fine Arts, with impressionist painters commanding most of his attention.

Beauford studied art in Boston from 1924 to 1929. He attended institutions such as the South Boston School of Art, Massachusetts Normal Art School, and the Copley Society, which offered evening classes. He found himself in New York after the stock market crashed, with the Great Depression closing in. But Beauford's time in New York contrasted its effects. He landed menial jobs and furthered his studies by attending the Art Students League. There he received instruction from Thomas Hart Benton and John French Sloan, the premier artist of the Ashcan movement. Beauford delighted in Harlem's art scene and became part of the Harlem Renaissance in the 1930s.

To promote his art, he created sketches of New York's elite citizens, and their positive reception led to Beauford working as a sketch artist at a Midtown dancing school owned by choreographer Billy Pierce. There, he painted professional dancers. Beauford was granted his first solo art exhibition in 1930 at the 135th Street branch of the New York Public Library, which featured five drawings created in pastels and ten drawings created in charcoal. His first major exhibition took place the same year when three of his portraits appeared in a group show at the Whitney Studio Galleries (now the Whitney Museum of American Art).

Beauford realized more art opportunities when he secured a part-time teaching position at a school in Greenwich Village. In time, he drifted downtown to the bohemian confines of

Portrait of Gaylord

A 1944 painting by Beauford Delaney. Oil on canvas mounted on artist board. Beauford Delaney enjoyed the company of famous writers and artists while he lived in New York. Many of them were subjects of his art. Some portraits featured talents that are unknown to the public today, such as this musician named Gaylord. Historians believe he was a pianist at a club frequented by Beauford, and one of his hands was missing two fingers.

Greenwich and set up a studio there. Beauford's creative output continued, as did his exhibitions, and he produced paintings of jazz musicians, socialites, urban landscapes, and street scenes featuring the poor of the city. His pieces were vibrant, with lively bursts of color that accentuated the subtle abstraction. While the work did not bring wealth or fame, it attracted an eclectic mix of acquaintances and friends. Among them were American writer Henry Miller, novelist and playwright William Saroyan, essayist Anaïs Nin, photographer Carl Van Vechten, and artists Alfred Stieglitz and Georgia O'Keefe.

Notable among his friends was writer and activist James Baldwin, who initially looked to Beauford as a mentor and father figure. The two met in 1940 when Baldwin was still in high school, and a lifelong friendship ensued. Beauford ultimately failed to achieve success in New York and often supported himself by obtaining steady jobs. At various times he worked as a telephone operator, bellhop, doorman, janitor, and caretaker. James Baldwin moved to Paris in 1948 to escape bigotry in America. Beauford visited Europe years later, first traveling to Rome, then, with the encouragement of Baldwin, to Paris in 1953, where he finally settled.

Two Expats

Beauford Delaney and his good friend James Baldwin, ca. 1960. Adapted from a photo courtesy of the Beauford Delaney estate.

In Paris, Beauford was free of the pressures of American life. That translated to freedom of expression in his art, which became increasingly abstract. Beauford resumed his friendship with James Baldwin and established new associations with other creative souls. But by the 1960s—while in poverty—Beauford's mental health deteriorated. He resorted to heavy drinking and suffered from paranoid delusions. Voices in his head also plagued him. Medical intervention and antidepressants led to a recovery of sorts, and Beauford returned to a life of painting, complete with a new studio made possible by caring friends.

In the early '70s, it was evident that Beauford no longer had control of his mental faculties. In 1975, he was committed to a sanitarium in Paris called Saint Anne's Hospital for the Insane, with James Baldwin acting as a primary trustee. Beauford steadily declined as time passed. He lost his memory and remained semi-conscious before dying on March 26, 1979. But his surviving works have received renewed interest and are on display in various art institutions across the American landscape. **U**

John W. Bubbles
The Father of Rhythm Tap

Banner image features John W. Bubbles overlooking 1930s Broadway in New York City.

John W. Bubbles developed a new tap dancing style because he wanted to infuse complexity into the form, and his innovation, which involved dropping the heels at offbeat intervals, was integral to rhythm tap. Born John William Sublett in Louisville, Kentucky in 1902, the nickname "Bubber"—which he altered slightly to "Bubbles"—stuck.

At age seven, Bubbles visited a theater for the very first time and wasn't impressed. He was so convinced he could sing better than anyone who appeared in the show, he headed backstage and said just that, which earned him a job in entertainment, leading to a lifelong career. He still did odd jobs on the side, as a batboy, stableboy, dishwasher, and peddler of coal, which he hauled using a goat he owned.

At age ten, Bubbles teamed up with another black six-year-old named Ford Lee Washington, whose nickname was "Buck." Taking the stage name Buck and Bubbles, the two won amateur shows and took their act on the road, performing in Louisville, Detroit, and New York. Bubbles sang and danced with Buck accompanying him while standing at a piano. Bubbles stopped singing at age eighteen when his voice changed, and he focused on dancing.

The new focus did not go well initially. Bubbles won some embarrassment

Buck and Bubbles

The song and dance team of Buck (Ford Lee Washington), right, and Bubbles (John William Sublett), are shown as they appeared in the early 1920s as top headliners at New York's Palace Theatre, the then mecca of vaudeville.

when he was laughed out of the Hoofer's Club in Harlem for letting his inexperience show. Eddie Rector and Dickie Wells, club veterans in attendance at the time, told Bubbles he was hurting the floor, then they booed the young tap dancer out the door. Bubbles headed west to California and worked on his tap-dancing routine for a year. When he returned to the Hoofer's Club, no one in the audience dared laugh when he debuted his double over-the-tops and triple back slides. Dancers often stole moves from one another in those days, so necessity forced Bubbles to innovate. In his book, *What the Eye Hears: A History of Tap Dancing*, author Brian Seibert quotes John Bubbles, who once said:

> I didn't want 'em to copy me, so when I did a show I never did the same step the same way. If I got four shows, I'd do it four different ways . . . I'd do new steps and I'd do old steps and turn them into something else."

Buck and Bubbles carried their vaudeville act to new heights, which reached a pinnacle in 1922 when they played the Palace Theatre in New York. Their live comedy act, which included singing and dancing, was so popular the duo headlined white vaudeville shows across the country. This made them a bigger draw than the Theatre Owners Booking Association (TOBA), which was the vaudeville circuit for black entertainers in the 1920s. This was a credit to their manager, acrobat Nat Nazarro, who discovered the two in New York.

In time, Buck and Bubbles appeared in several Broadway productions, including the 1935 opera *Porgy and Bess* composed by George Gershwin. Buck and Bubbles made history in other ways too, being the first blacks en-

Porgy and Bess

John W. Bubbles, Todd Duncan, and Anne Brown were part of the original cast.

gaged at Radio City Music Hall (according to the *New York Times*), and the first to perform at many theaters as they toured the country. Television appearances followed, and the two were among the first black performers to appear in broadcasts in the early days of television. The two appeared in various motion pictures as well, such as *Cabin in the Sky* (1943), *Atlantic City* (1944), and *A Song is Born* (1948). Buck passed away in 1955, and Bubbles was paralyzed after suffering a stroke in 1967. He died in 1996 at age 84. U

The Black Fives
The Pre-NBA Era of All-Black Basketball Teams

Banner image features the Alpha Physical Culture Club basketball team of the Black Fives Era.

After basketball emerged as a sport in 1891, its teams consisted of all-white players known as "fives," so-called for their five starting players. That remained the case for over a decade. But at the turn of the century, the sport entered black neighborhoods, and all-black teams began to form, as integration was still far off. These teams were called the "Negro fives, "colored quints," or "black fives." It is the era that produced the Harlem Globetrotters.

Before the 1950s, several dozen all-black basketball teams competed against one another in New York, Atlantic City, Pittsburgh, Philadelphia, Washington, D.C., Chicago, Cleveland, and other cities. In their final decade, the Black Fives also competed against white teams, and several Black Fives became world champions.

Tuberculosis, also called consumption, had ravaged the world in the nineteenth century, killing one in seven people. Americans were still dying from it in large numbers in the early 1900s. Blacks were particularly susceptible due to their subjection to poor living conditions in overcrowded urban neighborhoods. As a result, close to 25% of black Americans succumbed to tuberculosis in New York alone. An infectious bacterial disease that often affected the lungs, tuberculosis was usually treated by a stay in a sanatorium in the late-1800s, as it promised a healthful climate and lots of rest. But in 1904, a new strategy came into play in black communities.

That year, black athlete Conrad Norman founded the Alpha Physical Culture Club in Harlem and began organizing basketball games. Three years later, he formed a basketball team he called the Alpha Big Five, after the name of his new athletic club. And not only did Norman play on the team, but he also coached and managed a sister team called the New York Girls, which, in 1910, made history by becoming the nation's first independent all-black basketball team composed of females.

The New York Girls
And Conrad Norman.

The year Conrad Norman founded his athletic club in Harlem, some two hundred thirty miles away, a gym teacher named Edwin Bancroft Henderson introduced basketball to black students in segregated schools in Washington, D.C. The game soon entered various YMCAs, and in a matter of years, several all-black basketball teams sprang up throughout the country. In the ensuing decades, Black Fives teams were found as far as California and featured squads like the Los Angeles Red Devils, which boasted the legendary Jackie Robinson.

It is important to note that the era of the Black Fives was also the era of white supremacy, which meant that all-black teams could not play at venues reserved for whites only. Instead, they competed in segregated buildings: the dance floor of black ballrooms, church basements, meeting halls, and armories. Before and after the games, fans were allowed to dance to live music which spurred ticket sales. As time passed, the teams developed better organization, and competition between them culminated in the Colored Basketball World Championship, pitting the best teams against one another. The winningest team during the period was the New York Renaissance or New York Rens, with an overall record of 2588-539 over 30 years.

The New York Renaissance

Also called the New York Rens, the team played from 1922 to 1949.

Because the team was so dominant, officials invited New York Rens players to the first World Professional Basketball Tournament held in Chicago in 1939. The team faced off against the all-white Oshkosh All-Stars, who they defeated in the finals. That year, ten of the best all-white teams vied for the top spot, with only two all-black teams—the New York Rens and the Harlem Globetrotters—taking the court among the Black Fives.

The Rens' win over the Oshkosh All-Stars in the inaugural basketball tournament brought needed recognition to black players. Other Black Fives teams went on to win basketball tournaments over the next decade until the National Basketball Association (NBA) was formed and later integrated. Basketball began as a white sport and later entered black communities as an answer to disease. But as recently as the 2019–2020 season, the NBA roster skewed over 80% black and less than 18% white. Professional basketball is also among the most-watched sports in America, with several teams being worth billions of dollars apiece. Many of those valuable teams have since recognized the legacy of their predecessors, the Black Fives. **U**

The Chicago Defender
The Nation's Most Influential Black Newspaper

Banner image features a newsboy distributing the *Chicago Defender* in April 1942, superimposing a 1919 headline.

Robert S. Abbott

A later portrait of Robert adapted from a photo courtesy of the Chicago Literary Hall of Fame.

Founded on May 5, 1905, by Robert Sengstacke Abbott with an initial investment of only 25 cents, the *Chicago Defender* rose to become the most influential black newspaper in the country, and the most widely circulated among blacks. Self-proclaimed "The World's Greatest Weekly," the *Chicago Defender* made a lasting impact and reached a large readership well beyond the borders of its home city and state. Two-thirds of the paper's customers lived outside of Chicago. Abbott managed to extend its circulation by employing the services of Pullman porters who created a network of distribution along various train routes throughout the country and well into the slave South, where his paper was forbidden.

Abbott had all intentions of becoming a lawyer, but the law degree he received from Chicago's Kent College of Law in 1898 proved useless. He was unable to practice due to racial prejudice. Even valiant attempts at opening a private law firm in Gary, Indiana; Topeka, Kansas; and Chicago, Illinois failed. Abbott also did not pass the bar exam in Illinois. Before his interests shifted to the legal field, Abbott learned the printing trade, which he got a taste of in his youth when he worked as a printer's devil—an apprentice at a printing company. He was also inspired by his stepfather John Sengstacke, who launched a local paper, the *Woodville Times*, in 1889.

When he was 21, Abbott attended Hampton Institute in Virginia to learn the printing trade. He completed Hampton's printing course four years later, and the required academic work for a bachelor's in 1896. He worked as a part-time printer and teacher for a short period before enrolling at Kent College, but he returned to Chicago and the printing field when his legal venture fizzled. With 25 cents, Abbott managed a press run of 300 initial copies of the *Chicago Defender*. His headquarters was a small apartment owned by his landlady, Henrietta Plumer Lee. Abbott wrote, printed, and folded the four-page, six-column paper himself, then proceeded to distribute copies door-to-door throughout the growing black community in Chicago.

Three fairly successful black newspapers were already being published in Chicago—the *Broad Ax*, the *Conservator*, and the *Illinois Idea*—yet Abbott was determined to add his voice to the crowded mix. Newsstand sales would not come for another seven years. In the meantime, Abbott doggedly pursued newsworthy material, tirelessly solicited companies for advertising, and he enlisted others to aid in the distribution effort.

When the paper almost folded after its first few months in existence, Abbott's landlady, Henrietta, stepped in and moved Abbott's newspaper operation to the dining room of her apartment on the second floor of her State Street building. The *Chicago Defender* slowly bounced back, and as it grew, the operation swelled beyond the walls of the dining room and eventually encompassed the entire building at 3159 State Street. The building remained the paper's official headquarters for the next 15 years. In 1918, Abbott expressed his gratitude to Henrietta for her support by buying her an eight-room brick house.

The *Chicago Defender* was essentially a one-man printing press for several years, and Abbott was not able to pay himself a salary. Contributions by others were also unpaid, whether they came in the form of outside reporting, news items collected out-of-town, or the occasional editorial. Black railroad employees often gathered printed materials passengers left behind in the passenger cars, which Abbot culled for news that would interest his black readership. Things changed in 1910, the year Abbott was finally able to afford his first full-time employee, managing editor J. Hockley Smiley. Hockley's efforts helped the paper attract a wider audience, as the articles began to incorporate news related to the nation at large.

To sell more papers, articles were written in a militant and sensational manner, with bold headlines, graphic images, and red ink used to highlight racial injustice and inequality across the landscape. This was a tactic called yellow journalism. Lynchings, rapes, assaults, and all manner of evil inflicted on the black community were denounced in unmistakable language. Given its unapologetic approach, the paper was not supported by national distributors. Smiley proposed that Abbott enlist porters, theater people, and waiters to carry bundles of paper into the streets and throughout the country.

Despite the actions of the Klu Klux Klan, who attempted to seize bundles of the paper and threatened those who read it, the *Chicago Defender* was read insatiably by blacks in the slave South, its biggest market outside of Chicago. While it started at the bottom, the *Chicago Defender* soon outsold its three main rivals. By 1916, it was being distributed to 71 cities and towns across the country, and powerhouse writers like Ida B. Wells-Barnett (who covered lynchings and riots) were on staff. Abbott and Smiley also refashioned the *Chicago Defender*, extending the format to include sports, theater, society, and editorial departments, a first for a black newspaper. Another first was reaching a circulation of over 100,000 readers each week.

The paper's influence reached its full height during World War I, when, beginning on October 7, 1916, it launched a campaign to lure blacks from the South with an editorial page announcing, "Farewell, Dixie Land." This was a call for:

> every black man for the sake of his wife and daughter to leave even at a financial sacrifice every spot in the south where his worth is not appreciated enough to give him the standing of a man and a citizen in the community."

Hot off the Press

John H. Sengstacke and Charles P. Browning reviewing copies of the paper fresh off the printing press in 1944.

Many blacks in the South who read the *Chicago Defender* heeded the call. Between 1916 and 1919, between 200,000 and 400,000 blacks migrated to free states in the North in the Great Migration, over 100,000 descending on Chicago alone. This nearly tripled Chicago's black population by 1920. Throughout the ongoing campaign, articles in the paper pointed out the dangers blacks faced by remaining in the South while highlighting the benefits of living in the North.

As Abbott began to age, he looked to an heir to take the reins of the paper. He found one in his favored nephew John H. Sengstacke, who assumed control of the *Chicago Defender* in 1940 and furthered Abbott's vision. Among his many contributions, Sengstacke is noted for championing the cause of integration. In 1948, his efforts paid off, when President Harry S. Truman integrated the U. S. Armed Forces through an Executive Order.

A Season of Change

President Harry S. Truman (left), John H. Sengstacke (center), and Chicago mayor Richard J. Daley (right) in the 1956 Bud Billiken Parade. Photo courtesy of the Abbott–Sengstacke Family Papers/Chicago Public Library.

The fate of the paper was impacted when the ensuing Civil Rights movement ignited news coverage of black oppression and inequality throughout the country. With the mainstream media now focusing on black issues, black newspapers, like the *Chicago Defender*, saw a sharp dip in circulation. By the 1970s, the paper's readership dwindled to under 40,000. John Sengstacke stayed on as publisher until May 1997, the month he passed away. Upon his death, ownership passed to Sengstacke's heirs. But in 2003, the *Chicago Defender*, as well as its sister publications, were sold to Real Times Media, LLC, a company founded by a consortium of business leaders from Chicago and Detroit. 🅄

The Robert S. Abbott House

The house, built in 1900, is now a National Historic Landmark.

ack Nurses of Stillman House
A Bygone but Not Forgotten Settlement Era

Banner image features a group portrait of Lincoln School nurses, circa 1930.

At the turn of the twentieth century, a young black registered nurse named Elizabeth Tyler was ready to use her training, but she had no patients to treat. While black women had been hired as caretakers for both blacks and whites in various communities for some time, in this period, it was unheard of for black women to receive education for and be registered as nurses. In a rare turn, Elizabeth Tyler had received such an education, both from Freedmen's Hospital Training School for Nurses and the Lincoln School for Nurses, but despite this, she was not only restricted from treating white patients, but people of her own ethnicity didn't trust her.

Upon leaving the Lincoln School for Nurses, in 1906 she was hired as the first black visiting nurse by a wealthy Jewish woman named Lillian Wald, who founded The Henry Street Nursing Settlement on Manhattan's Lower East Side. Wald was a progressive woman, who at the time had allowed the first NAACP Convention to be held in the Henry Street dining room. Despite her bold move in hiring Tyler, however, finding patients for her to treat proved impossible. Not one to be outdone, Tyler decided to find her own patients. She headed uptown to the black neighborhood of San Juan Hill (now primarily the Lincoln Square neighborhood) and entered several tenements to directly engage with black residents in need of medical care, largely for tuberculosis and other infectious diseases, paralysis, and various ailments.

Having been pushed farther uptown from the Lower East Side in 1900, blacks settled the San Juan Hill neighborhood and swelled to about 10,000 in number. While San Juan Hill, which ran from roughly 40th to 65th Street at the time, is an exclusive neighborhood today—where rents can soar to $17,000 a

San Juan Hill
The neighborhood as it was, circa 1940. Photo courtesy of the New York Public Library.

month—it was quite different in pre-World War I days. Blacks suffered institutional racism in this period and high mortality rates plagued San Juan Hill, claiming the lives of many black mothers and their babies. White doctors and nurses didn't venture to that part of the city, which, according to an archived clipping of the *New York Amsterdam News*, was a neighborhood:

> ... where housing conditions bordered on a state of almost feudalism. Cold water flats with outside toilets renting for about $10 per month were not the exception but the general rule."

Initially, residents of San Juan Hill were also mistrustful of Elizabeth Tyler, and they refused to let her into their apartments. This forced Tyler to improvise by befriending the janitors of the various tenements, who granted her unprecedented access to potential patients. Tyler saw a sore need for another settlement house, which was a popular holdover from the nineteenth century, and an important means of supplying healthcare, education, and other services to poverty-stricken areas. She sought the aid of her wealthy benefactor, Lillian Wald, to establish a settlement in San Juan Hill, and Wald happily agreed. As Daphne Spain writes in her book, *How Women Saved the City*, the result was "a spinoff from" the Henry Street Settlement known as Stillman House, located at 154 West 62nd Street in Manhattan.

Medical Pioneers

Elizabeth Tyler and Edith Carter. Adapted from photos courtesy of the Henry Street Settlement Archives.

What began as a storefront, being operated by a handful of nurses that included Elizabeth Tyler, Edith Carter, and Jessie Sleet Scales, the Stillman House Settlement became a vital fixture of the community by offering health care and social services to San Juan Hill's black residents. Not only did the new settlement boast these black nurses who treated patients and provided needed care, but Stillman House eventually included a penny provident bank for the poor, classes in city history, carpentry and sewing services, a men's civic club, social clubs for all ages, a circulating library, and an open-air community playground for the children, according to the *Handbook of Settlements* published in 1911. While it existed, Stillman house was a needed boost to a community that had long been detached from the regeneration of the wider city. 🅄

Willa Beatrice Brown
Aviation Pioneer and Pilot-Maker

Banner image features Willa Beatrice Brown overlooking a Grumman Widgeon flown by Civil Air Patrol crewmen.

As with Bessie Coleman—who was her inspiration—Willa Beatrice Brown was a pioneer in her own right, earning her pilot's license in 1937, being the first black female to do so in the United States. Noted for being the first black American female to run for Congress, Willa also made history as the first black American officer of the official auxiliary of the United States Air Force, a federally-supported corporation known as the Civil Air Patrol (CAP).

Willa was born in Glasgow, Kentucky, in 1906, to an African American father and a mother of Native American descent. Early in life, Willa saw the importance of education, so she focused on her studies. After graduating from Wiley High School in Terre Haute, Indiana, she earned her bachelor's at Indiana State Normal School (now Indiana State University). Her master's degree came ten years later from Northwestern University. She taught high school in Gary, Indiana, before moving to Chicago. There she became a social worker. But being an aviator was still a fascination for Willa throughout the years.

Willa started taking flying lessons in 1934 as a sideline. Her career took a turn when she met a man named Cornelius Coffey, a certified flight instructor at a white-owned and segregated flight school. Not only did Willa train with him, but the two also co-founded a private flying academy—the Coffey School of Aeronautics—and got married. Willa soon joined two flight clubs, and eventually, she purchased a plane. Their flight school,

Cornelius Coffey

Explaining aviation to an unknown woman. Adapted from a photo courtesy of the National Air and Space Museum, Smithsonian Institution.

the first black-owned and operated one in America, trained roughly 200 pilots over seven years. A 1939 government contract made it possible, and the school won the contract to train pilots in preparation for a national emergency, given it was wartime. Many of Willa's students were members of the famed Tuskegee Airmen, part of the elite 99th Fighter Squadron known as the "Red Tails." As a result of these efforts, Willa was instrumental in the integration of the military.

Willa also fought for the inclusion of blacks in a pilot training program for civilians. To this end, she became a training coordinator and teacher for the Civil Aeronautics Administration and Civilian Pilot Training Program respectively. Ten years after her first flight, Willa flew planes as an aviation enthusiast, a civilian flight instructor, and a military officer. Indeed she had many firsts, including the distinction of being the first American woman of any race to have both a mechanic's and commercial pilot's license. In 1939, the government cited Willa in the 76th Congressional Record for her achievements in aviation. After ending her aviation career, Willa returned to teaching in high schools, and she did so from 1962 until she retired in 1971. **U**

Making it Official

Willa Beatrice Brown and several male colleagues at a swearing-in ceremony in 1942, making them officers of the Civil Air Patrol. Adapted from a photo courtesy of the Federal Aviation Administration, National Archives.

Black History Month
From Negro History Week to a Monthlong Celebration

Banner image features Carter G. Woodson and a Black History Month street celebration.

Black History Month as we know it was first observed in the second week of February since the birthdays of two notable black history figures (Abraham Lincoln and Frederick Douglass) occurred during that week. The concept of carving out time to reflect on the historical achievements of blacks rests with Harvard-educated historian Carter G. Woodson and other prominent figures in the black community. The idea began to stir in Woodson in 1915 when he traveled from Washington, D.C. to Chicago, Illinois, to attend a state-sponsored commemoration of the fiftieth anniversary of the emancipation of American blacks held at the Coliseum.

Thousands flocked to Chicago for the event, and many waited in line for their turn to view the exhibits, including Carter G. Woodson's black history display, since he was an exhibitor. Woodson attended the University of Chicago, from which he earned both a bachelor's and master's, and in 1912, he received his doctorate from Harvard. He was the second black person to receive a doctorate from Harvard University, after W.E.B. Du Bois. With his doctorate in hand, Woodson devoted himself to the study of black history. The three weeks he spent in Chicago, at the emancipation celebration, inspired him to redouble his efforts.

Even before he left Chicago, Woodson formed an organization dedicated to promoting the scientific study of black life and history. During the third week of the exhibit (on September 9, 1915), he went to the Wabash YMCA and met with its executive secretary, A.L. Jackson, a fellow Harvard alumnus. Also in attendance were George Cleveland Hall, a black physician and humanitarian, and James E. Stamps, a Yale graduate student whose focus was

The Wabash YMCA

A depiction of the 1925 Wabash Avenue YMCA, based on a photo courtesy of the New York Public Library.

economics. Together, they formed the Association for the Study of Negro Life and History (ASNLH).

Before the founding of the ASNLH, black scholars and historians had no professional outlets to foster and promote their ideas or accept them as members. To facilitate this, Woodson—together with Jesse E. Moorland, a minister and civic leader—launched the *Journal of Negro History* in 1916 through the University of Chicago Press. The journal became a printed forum for the presentation and spread of historical findings in black history research.

A decade later—that being February 1926—Woodson announced the first Negro History Week via a press release. There was overwhelming support for the celebratory week from the start. Both the public and schools across the country embraced the concept by observing the week. Black people far and wide were experiencing their culture in new ways and learning a great deal about their collective history. Even some whites supported the cause. But the success of the celebration soon gave way to exploitation, and it wasn't long before seasoned opportunists swooped in to reap financial rewards from unsuspecting knowledge-hungry patrons. Publishing houses, which largely ignored black content in the past, seized the moment and began churning out black history books to supply mainstream audiences and schools.

As the decades rolled, interest in authentic black history studies increased, and there was a push to expand its coverage in schools. By the 1940s, Negro History Week expanded to a monthlong celebration in select communities, and by the 1960s—in the midst of the civil rights movement and the rise of black consciousness—the monthlong celebration was becoming mainstream, particularly on college campuses. Then, in 1976, Carter G. Woodson's association (which dropped the Negro in its name and became the Association for the Study of African American Life and History) pushed for the widespread adoption of February as Black History Month. President Gerald R. Ford made the celebration official by calling on Americans to join in observing the month, saying:

> Seize the opportunity to honor the too-often neglected accomplishments of black Americans in every area of endeavor throughout our history."

Since President Ford, every successive president has appointed February as Black History Month. U

President Gerald R. Ford.

Ginger Smock
The Pioneering Jazz Violinist and Bandleader

Banner image features Ginger Smock and her instrument of choice.

Known for delivering blues-infused violin solos that carried harmonic structures akin to the horn, violinist Ginger Smock paved the way for other talented female musicians in a male-dominated industry. The jazz scene that developed in Los Angeles was shaped in part by Ginger's contribution, as she was an important trailblazer during the 1940s and '50s.

Emma Smock—nicknamed "Ginger"—was born in Chicago on June 4, 1920. With the untimely death of her parents, Ginger was orphaned at age six and sent to live with her aunt and uncle in a black community located on Central Avenue in Los Angeles, California. In the 1930s, Central Avenue became a thriving music scene for blacks, and it attracted big names like Nat "King" Cole, Duke Ellington, and Louis Armstrong. Ginger was adopted by her aunt and uncle, and they soon realized her nascent musical talent. Central Avenue families at the time had suffered the ill effects of racial discrimination, which barred them from certain career paths. This caused many of them to secure private music lessons for their children as a way of laying a foundation for success in the future.

To that end, Ginger's adoptive parents purchased a violin for her and eventually arranged for private studies with Bessie Dones, who taught her classical violin around the age of eight. Ginger proved to be a prodigy. A rare performance she gave at the Hollywood Bowl at age ten resulted in a standing ovation. While she attended Jefferson High School, she joined the school orchestra and even became a drum majorette on the marching band, which was led by celebrated black music teacher Sam Browne. Ginger became such an accomplished violinist that she later figured prominently in two musical organizations, the Los Angeles Junior Philharmonic—which

Ginger's Violin

The eventual violin she owned, said to have been the work of Ferdinand August Homolka, was created in 1849 in Prague, Czech Republic. Courtesy of the National Museum of African American History and Culture.

was composed primarily of whites, apart from her—and the All-City Stu
dent Symphony. Ginger became interested in jazz music when she heard i
on the phonograph and radio as a little girl, from the likes of jazz violinist:
Eddie South, Joe Venuti, and Stéphane Grappelli.

Many of the star players she grew up listening to she later met, includ
ing Stuff Smith, who launched her jazz career when she was called to sub
stitute for him at a jazz club in 1943. That same year Ginger, who formed :
female trio called the Sepia Tones with Mata Roy and Nina Russell, playe(
jazz around Southern California. And after World War II, Ginger rose t(
prominence in Los Angeles.

She began playing classy venues like the Cocoanut Grove in Santa Mon
ica. And she enjoyed an extended stint at the Waikiki Inn, where she performed with her band in Hawaiian outfits. A November 15, 1947 edition o1
the *Cleveland Call and Post* reports that, following a stunning performanc(
at a nightclub on Central Avenue called the Last Word, four clubs in Sar
Francisco started a bidding war to secure her services. Ginger was soor
tapped to record on composer Leonard Geoffrey Feather's album *Girls in
Jazz*, which was the first record to chronicle the work of female jazz musicians. Ginger also landed a job as a radio show host for *Melody Parade.*

Her television debut came in 1951
when Ginger and the Sepia Tones hosted a
thirty-minute TV show that aired on CBS
affiliate KTSL for six weeks. She also went
on to host a live television show of her own
in 1957 called *Rhythm Review*. Other recordings followed, and Ginger moved on to
other gigs, including a four-year stint on a
cruise ship that saw her leading a quartet.
This too led to a recording, the LP titled,
*On the S.S. Catalina with the Shipmates
and Ginger*. As time passed, the discrimination Ginger faced as both a black person

The Sepia Tones

and a woman led to fewer opportunities, with many of her jazz recordings
unreleased to the public. She spent the rest of her music career in the virtu-
al shadows, playing concertmaster for orchestras in Los Angeles and, later,
Las Vegas, where her venues were The Flamingo, The Sands, Ceaser's
Palace, and The Tropicana.

While the City of Los Angeles recognized her cultural contributions
with an award before she moved to Las Vegas, Ginger pursued the best
opportunity available to her in the desert, where she enjoyed life with her
husband. Toward the end of her life, she played little to no jazz but returned
to playing church music each week at Trinity Temple in Las Vegas. Ginger
died on January 1, 1995, at age 74. 🅤

Norma Merrick Sklarek
The First Licensed Black Female Architect

Banner image features Norma Merrick Sklarek and Commons-Courthouse Center which she co-designed in 1973.

Norma Merrick Sklarek's name was added to the annals of history when she became the first licensed black female architect in New York and California. In 1980, she was also the first black woman to be awarded a fellowship by the American Institute of Architects. Half a decade later, she made history again as a founder of the architectural firm Siegel, Sklarek, and Diamond, which was a partnership with Margot Siegel and Katherine Diamond. No other black woman before her had established and managed such a firm.

Norma Merrick Sklarek was born in Harlem, New York on April 15, 1926. Her parents were Dr. Walter Ernest Merrick and Amelia Willoughby, who worked as a seamstress. Walter and Amelia moved to Harlem from Trinidad, but after Norma was born they later settled in Brooklyn. Norma studied architecture at Columbia University and earned her

Harlem Hospital

The hospital as it stood in 1926. Adapted from a photo courtesy of the Schomburg Center for Research in Black Culture, NYPL.

historic degree in 1950. Aside from being the only black female architect in America, women on a whole made up a slim minority in the field. Only one white woman was in her graduating class.

After graduating, Norma was hired as a junior draughtswoman at the New York Department of Public Works, where she remained until 1954. While there, she applied to nineteen firms but was rejected by all of them. That year, her bosses pushed her to take the architecture exam. In doing so, Norma succeeded in becoming the first black female architect licensed in New York. When she applied to the next firm, Skidmore, Owings, and Merrill the next year, she was hired. She worked at Skidmore until 1960.

Norma became a single mother during this time, and her mother helped raise her two children while she worked during the day and taught evening classes in architecture at New York City Community College. After leaving Skidmore in 1960, Norma relocated to Los Angeles, California to work for Gruen Associates, where she experienced an upswing in her career. Two years after joining the new firm, she became a licensed architect in California, while retaining her license to practice architecture in New York. In 1975, Norma wrote to the vice-chancellor at the University of California at Los Angeles (UCLA), where she served on the faculty:

> As far as I know, I am the first and only black woman architect licensed in California. I am not proud to be a unique statistic, but embarrassed by our system which has caused my dubious distinction."

Norma was so adept in her field that by 1966, she was named director at Gruen, another first for a black American female. But her rise to prominence was met with its share of obstacles. In the male-dominated field of architecture, women were rarely acknowledged for their creative contributions. A black woman, albeit a director, had less of a chance of being recognized for their work. This was the case with Norma. Despite her collaboration on high-profile projects that included California Mart, San Bernardino City Hall, Columbus, Indiana's Commons Courthouse Center, and the U.S. Embassy in Tokyo, Japan between 1963 and 1976, design credit went to an architect from Argentina named César Pelli. Norma was seen as the project manager rather than the designer.

Despite the disregard for her creative efforts, Norma remained at Gruen Associates until 1980. That was the year she also became the first black female fellow of the American Institute of Architects. Norma then accepted a position at Welton Becket Associates, a firm that appointed her as project director for a construction project at Los Angeles International Airport. A new station at Terminal One was being built, which would cost $50 million and had to meet a completion date that landed in the first quarter of 1984 before the summer Olympics commenced. Norma would later say that, while many projects were underway as she was overseeing her own, male architects regarded her with skepticism because she was a black female. But construction of Terminal One was the only project at Los Angeles Interna-

Norma Merrick Sklarek

Pioneering female architect.

tional Airport that finished on schedule before summer.

Norma left Welton Becket Associates the year after her big project and co-founded Siegel, Sklarek, and Diamond, an all-female firm (one black, two white) that at the time was considered the largest such architecture firm in the U.S. Norma saw this move as the surest way to remove some of the obstacles present in her field and allow her to showcase her design skills, build a proper portfolio, and establish an impressive work history while receiving due credit.

Margot Siegel, Norma Merrick Sklarek, and Katherine Diamond

Norma joined another Los Angeles partnership in 1989 called JERDE, which, according to them, is:

> a diverse group of designers, architects, and thinkers who put people and experiences first."

Norma later taught at UCLA and became director of the University of Southern California Architects Guild. While she retired in 1992, she did not do so quietly. Norma was appointed to the California Architects Board by the governor and was chair of the National Ethics Council that was part of the American Institute of Architects. While at home in Pacific Palisades, California, Norma died of heart failure on February 6, 2012, at the age of 85. U

Roy Eaton
The Hall of Fame Composer in General Market Advertising

Banner image features Roy Eaton during his days on Madison Avenue.

R oy Eaton was a producer of popular advertising jingles that resonated with the public decades after the launch of the initial campaign. Many of his classic compositions can still be heard on nostalgic reruns airing on TV Land. Many can recall the Texaco classic: "You can trust your car to the man who wears the star," or the enduring Beefaroni ditty—

We're having Beefaroni.
Beef and macaroni.
Beefaroni's full of meat.
Beefaroni, what a treat.
Beefaroni's really neat.
Hooray, for Beefaroni!

The Beefaroni jingle, in particular, ran for more than twenty years, despite an executive's initial dislike of the song. The classic 1962 Texaco tune, on the other hand, was recognized by *Advertising Age* as a foundational component of the top 100 ad campaigns of the past century.

Roy Eaton was born in Harlem, New York on May 14, 1930. His parents were Felix and Bernice Eaton, a mechanic and domestic worker, respectively. Both were of Jamaican descent. At the age of three, Roy suffered a horrible accident that cost him a partial finger on his right hand. Despite the loss, he started taking classical piano lessons at age six and proved to be a piano prodigy. After a first-place win in a piano competition—the only one he ever entered—Roy played Carnegie Hall in 1937 at a mere seven years of age. He played piano for the rest of his life and built a successful career on the art form. But while his subsequent advertising efforts afforded a comfortable lifestyle, composing ad jingles is not a complete representation of his music career.

Roy attended the High School of Music and Art in New York and graduated in 1946. He thereafter enrolled in two schools: the City College of New York and the Manhattan School of Music. He studied history at the former and piano and musicology at the latter and graduated from both in 1950. Over the next two years, Roy studied at Yale University via a fellowship and earned a master's in musicology. While at Yale, Roy debuted with the Chicago Symphony Orchestra in 1951, where he performed Chopin. The next year, he performed Beethoven during his Town Hall debut in New York City.

Roy began a lifelong tenure at the Manhattan School of Music in 1952, as a concert pianist, performer, and lecturer. The Korean War commenced in 1950, and Roy was drafted into the U.S. Army in 1953. He served at a hospital radio station that operated out of Fort Dix near Trenton, New Jersey. For two years, Roy continued to write and produce radio programs, even after the U.S. pulled out of Korea.

He left the Army in 1955 and landed a job as a composer and copywriter at Young and Rubicam (Y&R), a New York advertising agency on Madison Avenue. In this role, Roy became the first black person to work for a major ad company with a direct hand on general accounts. At Y&R, Roy spent four years producing roughly seventy-five percent of the agency's entire music for ads. Brands included Gulf Oil, General Electric, Johnson & Johnson, Spic and Span, Beefaroni by Chef Boyardee, and Kent Cigarettes, for which Roy wrote a catchy tune about a new micronite filter that was considered safe at the time. In an interview with CNN, Roy stated:

Of course I have since discovered that the filtration process was accomplished by putting asbestos in the filter."

Madison Avenue, late 1950s

Roy came very near to death in 1957, after a fatal car crash that took the life of his new wife. He had been married less than a year. Doctors determined his odds of survival at ten percent and he was left in a coma. After recovering, Roy's faith deepened and he devoted himself to his work. In 1959, he moved to another advertising agency, Benton & Bowles, where he functioned as the music director. At Benton & Bowles, Roy produced music for many brands, including Hardee's, G.I. Joe, Mr. Potato Head, and Sugar Crisp cereal, which featured an anthropomorphic bear that sang a jingle Dean Martin style: "I can't get enough o' that Sugar Crisp!"

While there was rampant discrimination in the advertising industry, with various barriers in place that restricted entry to blacks, Roy's creative genius and determined work ethic allowed him to rise to the top. He became vice president of Benton & Bowles on January 3, 1968. Roy spent another twelve years at Benton & Bowles before leaving

The Piano Tuner

Roy Eaton enjoyed an impressive career that allowed him to grace the stages of cities throughout the world. He has run the gamut from playing Carnegie Hall as a child prodigy to graciously giving free concerts in New York City's Bryant Park. And aside from his catchy advertising jingles, Roy was the first-ever recipient of the Kosciuszko Foundation Chopin Award in 1950.

> *While there was rampant discrimination in the advertising industry, with various barriers in place that restricted entry to blacks, Roy's creative genius and determined work ethic allowed him to rise to the top.*

in 1980 to launch a music production company, Roy Eaton Music, where he served as president. Through his company, Roy produced music for large brands such as Coca-Cola and celebrities like Michael Jackson. Roy also embarked on a classical music career and has since graced international concert stages performing the music of George Gershwin, Scott Joplin, Frédéric Chopin, and others.

Roy was inducted into the American Advertising Federation's Advertising Hall of Fame on March 26, 2010. He remarried and fathered five sons. He and his wife settled on Roosevelt Island in New York with their twin boys, Ari and Ravi, and Roy continues to inspire listeners with his classical performances. **U**

Jews and Black Schools
How HBCUs Saved Jewish Scholars from the Nazis

Banner image features Professor Georg Iggers, James E. Shepard, and Howard University.

W hen poring over details of World War II, scholars noticed striking similarities between the Jews in Nazi Germany and blacks in the American South: both experienced racism and terror. Through Jim Crow laws, blacks were legally discriminated against and racially oppressed. In January 1933, Adolph Hitler and the Nazi Party likewise rose to power in Germany through legal and democratic means. Following that, they implemented a systematic campaign of oppression against Germany's Jewish population. In a matter of months, Jewish intellectuals and educators who held prestigious posts in Germany's universities faced immediate expulsion. These scholars attempted to flee Germany, and the United States was an attractive option. But gaining entry was not a simple matter.

U.S. officials believed Jewish refugees would weigh down the economy through their dependence on the government for subsistence, so they had to prove they could support themselves once they settled in the country as part of the public charge rule. Many Jews abandoned their homes and livelihoods to escape imprisonment and death, so they had little money. The Nazis largely confiscated Jewish properties and wealth. That left a sizable portion of Jews ineligible for obtaining a U.S. visa. Some Jews managed to secure affidavits from relatives who were U.S. citizens. Their promise of support aided in the application process, but long waiting lists and the overall immigration policy proved an arduous ordeal.

A few private organizations in the U.S. recognized the problem and intervened. One committee, the American Friends Service, even enlisted individuals with no relation to the Jewish immigrants to

Barriers to Entry

A Jewish couple seeks refugee assistance while a staff member helps them with their immigration papers.
Photo courtesy of the JDC Archives.

commit to supporting them upon their arrival. As part of that effort, the Emergency Committee in Aid of Displaced Foreign Scholars—formed by the Rockefeller Foundation—aimed to place former Jewish academics from German universities at universities in the U.S. on work visas. While that sounded good in theory, American universities were reluctant to hire Jews. Established faculty members at schools throughout the country viewed the refugees as a threat since new salaries had to flow to the incoming scholars.

College administrators often wielded power to hire these Jewish professors. But the only administrators who did so were the ones at historically black colleges and universities (HBCUs), who empathized with the Jewish experience of discrimination and oppression. Fifty-three Jewish scholars fleeing Nazi Germany received jobs and work visas from HBCUs like the North Carolina Central University in Durham (NC Central), Tougaloo College in Mississippi, and Howard University in Washington, D.C. Those black institutions, in effect, saved the lives of 53 Jews who had been turned away from white, prestigious schools in the U.S. One noted Jewish scholar, Ernst Manasse, who taught at NC Central from 1939 to his retirement in 1973, said:

> If I had not found a refuge at that time, I would have been arrested, deported to a Nazi concentration camp, tortured and eventually killed."

NC Central's black president James E. Shepard hired Ernst just before his work visa expired. Shepard also hired three other Jewish refugees. Many of the Jewish professors had never encountered black people, and neither had many students been among Jews, segregation being what it was. But the Jewish professors developed a rapport with the black students based on a shared experience. Being able to witness firsthand what blacks suffered in the South gave the Jewish scholars a window into something with which they were intimately familiar. Through their interaction, an interesting

College administrators often wielded power to hire these Jewish professors. But the only administrators who did so were the ones at historically black colleges and universities (HBCUs).

discourse emerged. Some students were struck by the idea that America dispatched troops across the Atlantic to fight Nazis when Jim Crow existed in the South. Professors like Georg Iggers agreed. He was a Jewish refugee from Germany who taught at Philander Smith College, another historically black institution. He said of his experience in the South:

> Racial segregation reminded me a lot of Nazi Germany, except that I wasn't a victim, the black population was."

Jessye Norman
The Celebrated Soprano and International Opera Sensation

Banner image features Jessye Norman doing what she did best. Based on a photo courtesy of Sergei Chirikov/EPA.

Jessye Norman credited black opera singers before her with paving the way for her success. Marian Anderson is among them. Jessye Norman, like Anderson, was able to sing French and German operas in the classical style, and her vocal charisma carried her to the stages of notable opera houses around the world. She also cultivated her career in Europe, where black artists were afforded far greater opportunities than in the United States, which was rampant with racism. Despite it all, Jessye gave command performances in operas, recitals, and concerts, and won multiple Grammy Awards, including one for lifetime achievement.

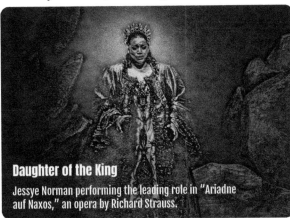

Daughter of the King

Jessye Norman performing the leading role in "Ariadne auf Naxos," an opera by Richard Strauss.

Jessye insisted on doing things her way, and she carved out a singing career that included an eclectic repertoire and a broad range of roles in various operas. Jessye gave back to her community in Augusta, Georgia as well, by founding a school for the arts there. And having endured racism throughout her life, she became a vocal civil rights advocate.

Jessye, though a prominent black artist in the classical world, faced racism in her industry, along with other black artists, yet she refused to cater to the whims of bigoted controllers. In her memoir, *Stand Up Straight and Sing!*, Jessye writes:

> Consider that a major network thought it a fine idea to invite me to play a role in a sitcom pilot about three maids who take the bus to work in the suburbs of Chicago. It is important to note that at that moment, my stage work consisted of roles where the lead was that of a queen of a country, as Alceste, Dido, Jocasta, and so forth."

Not only did she play queens onstage, but she also rubbed shoulders with real-life monarchs and heads of state. Jessye Norman was born on September 15, 1945, in Augusta, Georgia, to Janie King Norman, an amateur pianist, and Silas Norman, Sr., an insurance broker. Jessye grew up in a segregated world, where she was told by her mother that she was not allowed to play in a section of a Georgia train station that was for whites only. In a 2014 interview, she told NPR:

> I had a lot of questions about the segregation of the races when I was a young child and I still do."

Jessye held a bachelor's degree in music which she earned from Howard University, and she also studied at the University of Michigan and Peabody Institute. Throughout her singing career, Jessye developed a rich, voluptuous operatic voice that filled auditoriums with the full resonance of a majestic soprano. Peter Gelb, general manager of New York's Metropolitan Opera said that Jessye Norman was:

The Future is Bright
Jessye Norman at age 13.

> one of the greatest artists to ever sing on our stage."

The power of her voice penetrated the hearts of her audience, and she effortlessly sang the classical notes of concert arias fully fleshed, with the graceful accompaniment of the pit orchestra. It can be argued that Jessye Norman had no equal in the 1980s, during her prime years, which was the peak of her career. She sat on the board of several institutions, among them Carnegie Hall, the Dance Theatre of Harlem, City-Meals-on-Wheels in New York City, the New York Botanical Garden, the New York Public Library, and the National Music Foundation. She was also a member of the board of trustees for the Augusta Opera Association and of Paine College.

Jessye received numerous prestigious awards and distinguished honors in her career. Complications arising from a spinal cord injury she suffered in 2015 led to her death on September 30, 2019. Septic shock and multi-organ failure were cited as the cause of death. Two months later, Jessye was memorialized with a gala tribute at New York's Metropolitan Opera, the very opera house where she sang more than 80 performances. **U**

Mark Dean
The Groundbreaking Inventor and Computer Engineer

Banner image features Mark Dean and an early IBM computer from the IBM Corporate Archives.

Few have heard of Mark Dean, but his inventions have changed the world we live in. Mark—along with co-inventor Dennis Moeller—created a microcomputer system called Industry Standard Architecture (ISA). ISA is a computer bus protocol developed in the 1980s for 8-bit and 16-bit systems compatible with IBM. The addition of the ISA bus allowed peripheral processing devices attached to a motherboard to communicate with other devices attached to the same motherboard. The potential of the personal computer grew by leaps and bounds via ISA, as users could access ISA slots to add peripherals like printers, modems, video cards, speakers, scanners, disk drives, and other devices, therefore expanding the limits of Information Technology.

Mark E. Dean was born on March 2, 1957. His place of birth was the town of Jefferson City in eastern Tennessee, home to around 4,500 people at the time. But the town's black population was minuscule. Mark's parents were Barbara and James Dean. While his mother's side of the family had lived in Tennessee for several generations, his father spent his early years on a farm outside Mobile, Alabama. James Dean served in the Korean War and moved to Jefferson City to find work. He was hired onto a maintenance crew for the Tennessee Valley Authority and rose to become a dam supervisor by his early forties. He oversaw a crew that fixed electrical equipment and worked on big turbines and spillway gates. James brought Mark along on work trips at times, and Mark got to see the dam engineers in action, which fascinated him.

Mark admired his father for his mechanical skills. James Dean successfully rebuilt a 1931 Dodge and a 1947 Chevy, and together, he and his son built an entire tractor

The Car Builder
Mark Dean and his hand-built AC Cobra replica.

from scratch. Mark later said of his father:

> There was nothing I was aware of that he couldn't figure out. If he had grown up in my generation, he would have been an engineer."

Mark's grandfather was the principal of a small K-12 school named Nelson Mary. It was segregated and catered to very few students. Mark attended the school in childhood, sitting in a single classroom that served grades one to four. He was so advanced in his studies he found the math lessons to be extremely easy. Mark recalled that:

> One day, in first grade, I came home with a trigonometry book—at least, I remember it was a trigonometry book—and my mother called the teacher and asked if she had made a mistake. But I was already tutoring the fourth graders. It was easy for me. It felt so natural."

For Mark, English—be it reading or writing—was much more difficult to grasp. English had dozens of characters that were strung together to form words via a spate of complex rules. He admitted he struggled with the subject even in adulthood. But math consisted of ten digits and four operations he could make sense of. By the time he reached third grade, Jefferson City integrated its public schools so Mark no longer attended Nelson Mary. But due to the town's small black population, Mark was the only black student in all his classes into his high school years.

While he excelled in math, to the annoyance of some of his teachers, white students were perplexed by Mark's keen grasp of the subject. In middle school, Mark recalled a white friend coming up to him and asking if he was really black because he seemed too smart to be of that ethnicity. While he experienced bigotry growing up, Mark's parents encouraged him to join integrated sports teams, where he mixed with white teammates and treated them fairly. Before he graduated from middle school, Mark had decided to become an engineer. In high school, he decided to focus on computers, and he would attempt to pursue a career in that field by joining IBM.

After high school, Mark attended the University of Tennessee on a scholarship. He continued to earn stellar grades in college, except for two required English courses. In 1979, Mark graduated at the top of his class regardless and received a bachelor's in electrical engineering. He went on to earn a master's and a PhD in electrical engineering as well, from Florida Atlantic University (1982) and Stanford (1992). With his bachelor's in hand, Mark started interviewing with several corporations that interested him. Hewlett-Packard was one of those companies, and they were so impressed with Mark they offered him a job immediately. But Mark's heart was still set on IBM.

Shortly after graduating from the University of Tennessee, Mark headed to Boca Raton, Florida, which was the home of the IBM office complex at the time. Mark's first assignment while working at the tech hub was developing an adapter for a word processor that allowed letters and numbers to appear as graphics on the IBM Datamaster terminal screen—the Datamaster was an inexpensive computer that launched in July 1981. This led to Mark joining the IBM personal computer (PC) team and his efforts in helping to design IBM's first PC. To this end, Mark holds three core patents out of nine on which the PC is based, making him co-inventor of the landmark technology. Two of his three early patents are for adapters related to monochrome and color graphics.

Life at IBM

Mark Dean at IBM in the 1980s, when he was part of the PC development team.

At age 25, Mark became the lead on the ISA project, which created an entire PC ecosystem that became the industry standard due to its efficiency and simplicity. The introduction of the ISA bus system also gave the PC the edge over Apple. Mark created more groundbreaking inventions associated with the PC in the next few years, all of which made the computer more powerful and accessible. Mark's efforts produced the color monitor. In the late 1990s, Mark moved to Austin, Texas, to lead an engineering team at IBM's lab in developing the first gigahertz chip. Able to achieve a billion cycles per second, the new chip allowed central processing units to retrieve instructions, interpret them, and complete various tasks at vastly higher clock speeds than the previous multi-megahertz generation of microprocessors.

For his many achievements, Mark became the first black American to be named an IBM Fellow in 1995. In the words of IBM:

> The title of IBM Fellow is the company's pre-eminent technical distinction, granted in recognition of outstanding and sustained technical achievements and leadership in engineering, programming, services, science, design and technology."

Two years later, Mark was inducted into the National Inventors Hall of Fame. In 2013, Mark's life took a 360-degree turn when he became a professor of computer science and engineering at the very university from which he received his bachelor's in engineering more than three decades earlier. Many may not have heard of Mark E. Dean, but his inventions are in use each day. 🔲

1967: The Summer of Riots
A Brief Look Back

Banner image features National Guardsmen pushing back Michigan citizens from a burning building in Detroit.

Civil unrest erupted on a wide scale during the summer of 1967. Racial tensions reached a fever pitch and exploded into violence in several major American cities. It was dubbed "the Long, Hot Summer," and streets were filled with rioting amid burning buildings as blacks and whites clashed over issues that still plague black people today.

Civil Unrest

A reverend assesses the damage caused by riots in a Brooklyn neighborhood on July 23, 1964.

The outbreaks of violence that erupted in 1967 could be traced back to 1964. On July 18 of that year, six days of rioting ensued after a black teenager was shot and killed by a white off-duty police officer. Following the Harlem violence, rioting spread to other New York neighborhoods, including Bedford-Stuyvesant, Brooklyn's Brownsville, and South Jamaica, Queens. The year 1964 also marked the first in which race riots erupted in major American cities. Like an unseen epidemic, the spirit of violence and rioting of 1964 soon reached Rochester, New York; three cities in New Jersey; Dixmoor (near Chicago), Illinois; and Philadelphia.

More riots erupted in other northern urban areas of the United States into 1966, including the notorious 1965 Watts riots; the 1966 riots on Chicago's West Side; Cleveland, Ohio's Hough neighborhood; and Detroit, Michigan. This activity led directly to the violent disturbances of 1967. Ironically, 1967 was also deemed the Year of Love by white youths of the present counterculture who converged in San Francisco. In the west, white youths expressed free love, and psychedelic drugs and rock 'n' roll defined their era. The picture was quite different for blacks struggling to survive in the east. They forcibly endured the brutality of racist police, undesirable living conditions, and rampant, institutionalized unemployment.

The east was bound to see an explosive release of pent-up resentment sooner or later, but it came to full fruition in the summer. For nine agonizing months, culminating in September 1967, 34 U.S. states experienced a vicious cycle of violence and disorder. Over a hundred cities saw a wave of rioting, street fighting, looting, and chaos. City blocks became ruins, thousands were injured, and over 80 people lost their lives. As stated in our article on the Newark Riots, Lyndon B. Johnson launched an inquiry into the cause of the widespread disorder, which was the Kerner Commission, or Report. It found that:

> white racism is essentially responsible for the explosive mixture which has been accumulating in our cities since the end of World War II."

The report centered that racism on police practices, which were at the heart of the turmoil that stretched at times for days on end. The findings of the inquiry were spot on, but no one paid it any serious attention. Discrimination, segregated education, employment, and housing received blame for creating large concentrations of ghettos in black communities:

> where segregation and poverty converge on the young to destroy opportunity and enforce failure."

While the Kerner Commission pinpointed systemic problems at the core of American society, white citizens ignored those findings, instead opting for police to be armed to the teeth like military personnel. And this is what we see today. So the Newark riots, and all the riots before it, changed American policing in some ways, while many things, including racial disparity, remain the same. Riots are still being seen in America today for this reason. Ⓤ

The Civil Disorder Task Force
President Lyndon B. Johnson and members of the Kerner Commission.

Sesame Street's Blackness
How Harlem Influenced the Iconic Show

Banner image features the 1970 cast of *Sesame Street*. Based on a photo courtesy of TV critic Aaron Barnhart.

For more than half a century, the children's television program *Sesame Street* has been beaming into the households of hundreds of millions of viewers throughout the world. The show's popularity has grown to a point where, in 2018, it was estimated that close to one-third of all Americans (86 million people) had watched the series during their childhood. *Sesame Street*, having won close to 200 Emmy Awards, is the most decorated children's program in television history. In his book *Street Gang: The Complete History of Sesame Street*, writer Michael Davis declared the series an American institution by the mid-1980s, and it remains so today. But what many people do not know about *Sesame Street* is that, according to a *New York Times* article published ten years after its launch:

> the 'target child' was the 4-year old, inner-city, black youngster."

Family Viewing

Military families take in a special message from Elmo, a *Sesame Street* Muppet, in December 2011. Original photo credit: U.S. Army.

David D. Connell, former vice president for production, also added:

> The focus at the time was on the urban ghetto. Project Head Start had just been born of the same sense of urgency."

The kernels of the idea for *Sesame Street* formed during the Civil Rights era. President Lyndon B. Johnson had launched the Great Society initiative, which was an expansive reform plan that included policies, legislation, and programs aimed at eradicating poverty, lowering crime, and countering racial inequality. At the center of the education reform portion was Project Head Start, the brainchild of Johnson and several child development experts. Through the program, Johnson intended to extend early education to poor children in urban communities.

Head Start drew the attention of television producer Joan Ganz Cooney. A proponent for Civil Rights and education, Joan created a Head Start training film for teachers which aired on Channel Thirteen. Titled *A Chance at the Beginning*, the film featured intervention measures used on at-risk Harlem preschoolers. In 1966, Joan threw a winter dinner party in her New York apartment located half a block from Gramercy Park. One of the guests was Lloyd Morrisett, the future CEO of Carnegie Corporation. Morrisett was in charge of education research at the time and was on the hunt for a preschool program that was targeted at a large number of inner-city children.

Michael Davis said of that pivotal get-together:

> Before good nights were exchanged, the fates of Joan Ganz Cooney and Lloyd Morrisett had become entwined like strands of DNA. A professional relationship that spanned five decades started with Morrisett's ostensibly simple question, 'Do you think television could be used to teach young children?'"

Joan responded that she did not know, but was willing to discuss it. What resulted was the Children's Television Workshop (CTW), a production company of which Joan was made executive director on February 15, 1968. Morrisett was also able to raise $8 million in funding from federal and private support, including the Carnegie Corporation, the Ford Corporation, and the Corporation for Public Broadcasting. With the use of those funds, the CTW went on to produce *Sesame Street*.

Rebranded as Sesame Workshop in 2000, the CTW was a fitting sponsor for *Sesame Street*. It consisted of a production team that included television producers, writers, and directors, as well as a bevy of experts across the fields of education, psychology, child development, social sciences, advertising, and other areas. These experts were on hand to advise the administrative and creative teams as needed. As executive director, Joan was often surrounded by such advisors, some of whom were black educators

Joan and Company

Children's Television Workshop executor director Joan Ganz Cooney (second from left) is surrounded by black female advisors. Seated left to right are Jane O'Connor, Dorothy Hollingsworth, Allonia Gadsden, and Gwen Peters. Based on a photo courtesy of *Ebony* magazine.

with an awareness of the various issues that were of importance to urban blacks.

Dr. Chester Pierce—founding president of the Black Psychiatrists of America, and a professor of early childhood education—was concerned about the ill effects television had on young minds. As a black Harvard professor with this perspective, he was instrumental in helping to establish a foundational curriculum for the new preschool show tailored to low-income families, particularly inner-city blacks. Serving as a senior advisor, Dr. Pierce's contributions resulted in an integrated cast and strong black role models like teacher Gordon Robinson and his wife Susan, who were leading characters during the first season. The Gordon family became a fixture on the show and expanded while other human characters were sidelined in favor of more diverse Muppets.

The set for *Sesame Street* developed in 1968 as a result of a televised public service announcement (PSA) shot in Harlem. Producer Jon Stone was hired to create a sales film that would act as a fitting preview for the series currently in development. But he had so little to work with, he was bereft of ideas for the set design. As the TV spot ran, a sensational message flashed on-screen:

Send your kid to a ghetto this summer."

This was followed by a Harlem street scene (shot in the spring of 1968), with black actor Lincoln Kilpatrick leading viewers on a tour of the neighborhood. He mockingly referred to fire hydrants as pools, and streets lined with cars where kids played stickball were called ballfields. Field trips depicted dirty lots strewn with trash and cozy camp cabins were crowded inner-city apartment bedrooms, where three to four black children were packed into a bed. Kilpatrick ended his travelogue by saying:

You don't want your kids to play *here* this summer? Then don't expect ours to."

The TV spot closes by asking viewers to give jobs, money, and care to the cause. Jon Stone was inspired. In the book *Street Gang*, he explained his immediate takeaway:

> For a preschool child in Harlem, the street is where the action is. . . . Our set had to be an inner-city street, and more particularly it had to be a brownstone so the cast and kids could 'stoop' in the age-old New York tradition. . . ."

Stone met with a friend the next day, a set designer named Charles Rosen. Rosen was currently working on a feature film and led Stone on a tour of the studio. Stone marveled at the impressive touches designers and artists made to a set that served as the backstage room of a jazz club. Though the materials used to build it were new, they had been aged and distressed to make the club look like a dive. The designers spared no details in making the artificial grit look authentic. Stone decided then and there that he wanted a movie set along these lines for the new preschool show that would emerge as *Sesame Street*. No television set with the usual cardboard and canvas backdrops would do. Stone told Rosen:

Stoop Time

Educator and actress Loretta Long as Susan stands left. She is pictured with children on the stoop of the familiar *Sesame Street* brownstone. Based on a photo courtesy of *Ebony* magazine.

> I want it to be as real as this room, and I want you to design and build it."

With that, Rosen went forth scouting locations throughout Harlem and nearby neighborhoods, of which he took various photographs and drew sketches. The result was the familiar brownstone at 123 Sesame Street millions of viewers have come to know and love. **U**

Banner image features a bookshelf laden with old books.

Ater, Renée. *Remaking Race and History: The Sculpture of Meta Warrick Fuller.* Berkeley: University of California Press, 2011.

Athearn, Robert G. *In Search of Canaan: Black Migration to Kansas, 1879-80.* Lawrence: The Regents Press of Kansas, 1978.

Bacon, Jacqueline. *The First African-American Newspaper: Freedom's Journal.* Lanham, MD: Lexington Books, 2007.

Block, Melissa. "Here's What's Become of a Historic All-Black Town in the Mississippi Delta." *NPR*, National Publica Radio, Inc., 8 Mar. 2017, npr.org/2017/03/08/515814287/heres-whats-become-of-a-historic-all-black-town-in-the-mississippi-delta.

Brown, Alan S. "Mark E. Dean: From PCs to Gigahertz Chips," *The Bent of Tau Beta Pi*, spring 2015.

Cox, Anna-Lisa. *A Stronger Kinship: One Town's Extraordinary Story of Hope and Faith.* New York: Little, Brown and Company, 2006.

Cox, Bette Yarbrough. *Central Avenue: Its Rise and Fall, 1890–c. 1955: Including the Musical Renaissance of Black Los Angeles.* Los Angeles: BEEM Publications, 1996.

Davis, Michael. *Street Gang: The Complete History of Sesame Street.* New York: Penguin, 2009.

Fouché, Rayvon. *Black Inventors in the Age of Segregation: Granville T. Woods, Lewis H. Latimer, and Shelby J. Davidson.* Baltimore: The Johns Hopkins University Press, 2003.

Hechinger, Fred M. "About Education: Sesame Street After 10 Years." *New York Times*, 6 Nov. 1979: C5. Print.

Henderson, D.L. *South-View: An African American City of the Dead.* Dunwoody, GA: Carrelspin Press, 2018.

Hudson, Karen E. *Paul R. Williams, Architect: A Legacy of Style.* New York: Rizzoli, 1993.

Kinch, Michael. *Between Hope and Fear: A History of Vaccines and Human Immunity.* New York: Pegasus Books, 2018.

Kuska, Bob. *Hot Potato: How Washington and New York Gave Birth to Black Basketball and Changed America's Game Forever.* Charlottesville: University of Virginia Press, 2006.

Leeming, David. *Amazing Grace: A Life of Beauford Delaney.* New York: Oxford University Press, 1998.

Lupold, John, and Thomas L. French. *Bridging Deep South Rivers: The Life and Legend of Horace King.* Athens: The University of Georgia Press, 2019.

Marlowe, Gertrude Woodruff. *A Right Worthy Grand Mission: Maggie Len Walker and the Quest for Black Economic Empowerment.* Washington, D.C. Howard University Press, 2003.

Meehan, Thomas A. "Jean Baptiste Point du Sable, the First Chicagoan." *Journa of the Illinois State Historical Society (1908–1984),* vol. 56, no. 3, autumn 1963, pp. 439–453.

Metcalf McConnell, Miantae. *Deliverance Mary Fields, First African American Woman Star Route Mail Carrier in the United States: A Montana History* Columbia Falls, MT: Huzzah Publishing, 2016.

Nieto, Natalia Torija. "Remembering Norma Merrick Sklarek, an Architect of Man Firsts." *PIN-UP Magazine,* FEBU Publishing, LLC, 15 Apr. 2019, pinupmag azine.org/articles/article-norma-merrick-sklarek-first-liscensed-black-wom an-architect-new-york-california-natalia-torija.

Norman, Jessye. *Stand Up Straight and Sing!.* Boston: Mariner Books, Houghto Mifflin Harcourt, 2015.

Piascik, Andy. "Edward Alexander Bouchet: The First African American to Earn a PhD from an American University." *ConnecticutHistory.org,* Connecticu Humanities, 12 Feb. 2020, connecticuthistory.org/edward-alexander-bouchet the-first-african-american-to-earn-a-phd-from-an-american-university.

Proper, David R. "Lucy Terry Prince: 'Singer of History,' " *Contributions in Blacl Studies* Vol. 9, Article 15, 1992.

Rae, Noel. *The Great Stain.* New York: Abrams Press, 2018.

Report of the National Advisory Commission on Civil Disorders. [Washington United States], Kerner Commission: U.S. G.P.O., 1968.

Rhodes, Jane. *Mary Ann Shadd Cary: The Black Press and Protest in the Nine teenth Century.* Bloomington: Indiana University Press, 1998.

Schechter, Patricia. *Ida B. Wells-Barnett and American Reform: 1880–1930* Chapel Hill: University of North Carolina Press, 2003.

Schmitzer, Jeanne Cannella. *The Black Experience at Mammoth Cave, Edmon son County, Kentucky, 1838–1942.* 1994. University of Central Florida, M.A thesis. *Retrospective Theses and Dissertations,* stars.library.ucf.edu/rtd/3076

Seibert, Brian. *What the Eye Hears: A History of Tap Dancing.* New York: Farrar Straus and Giroux, 2015.

Shumacker, Harris B. *The Evolution of Cardiac Surgery.* Bloomington: Indiana University Press, 1992.

Tucker, Phillip Thomas. *Cathy Williams: From Slave to Female Buffalo Soldier.* Mechanicsburg, PA: Stackpole Books, 2002.

Tye, Larry. *Rising from the Rails: Pullman Porters and the Making of the Black Middle Class.* New York: Henry Holt and Co., 2004.

Walpole, Ford. "Edisto Island." *South Carolina Encyclopedia,* University of South Carolina, Institute for Southern Studies, 17 May 2016, scencyclopedia.org/ sce/entries/edisto-island.

Williams, Jean Kinney. *Bridget "Biddy" Mason: From Slave to Businesswoman.* Minneapolis, MN: Compass Point Books, 2006.

Winkler, Lisa K. "The Kentucky Derby's Forgotten Jockeys." *Smithsonian Mag azine,* the Smithsonian Institution, 23 Apr. 2009, smithsonianmag.com/histo ry/the-kentucky-derbys-forgotten-jockeys-128781428.

Index

Banner image features the old index card filing system.

NEWSLETTER

Sign up for our newsletter and immerse yourself in hidden black history.

Scan the QR code using the camera on your smartphone or tablet and . . .

STAY INFORMED

CPSIA information can be obtained
at www.ICGtesting.com
Printed in the USA
LVHW071823101121
702988LV00005B/176